Creating a Strategic Human Resources Organization

last
function   Service   shared   NOT shared

Creating a Strategic Human Resources Organization

An Assessment of Trends and New Directions

Edward E. Lawler III and Susan Albers Mohrman
with Alice Yee Mark, Beth Neilson, and Nora Osganian

Center for Effective Organizations
Marshall School of Business
University of Southern California

*A CEO report of a study funded by the Human Resource Planning Society
and the corporate sponsors of the Center for Effective Organizations*

STANFORD UNIVERSITY PRESS
STANFORD, CALIFORNIA 2003

Stanford University Press
Stanford, California
© 2003 by the Board of Trustees of the
Leland Stanford Junior University

Printed in the United States of America
on acid-free, archival-quality paper

Special discounts for bulk quantities of Stanford
Business Books are available to corporations,
professional associations, and other organizations.
For details and discount information, contact the
special sales department of Stanford University Press.
Tel: (650) 736-1783, Fax: (650) 736-1784

Library of Congress Cataloging-in-Publication Data
Lawler, Edward E.
    Creating an effective human resources
organization : trends and new directions /
Edward E. Lawler III, Susan Albers Mohrman;
with Alice Yee Mark, Beth Neilson, Nora Osganian.
        p.   cm.
    Includes bibliographical references.
    ISBN 0-8047-4702-4 (pbk. : alk. paper)
    1. Personnel management.   2. Personnel
departments.   3. Human capital.   4. Organizational effectiveness.   5. Personnel management—
Technological innovations.   6. Personnel
management—Computer network resources.
I. Mohrman, Susan Albers.   II. Title.
HF5549 .L288   2003
658.3—dc21   2002153930

Original Printing 2003
Last figure below indicates year of this printing:
11   10   09   08   07   06   05   04   03
Typeface: 10½/14 Palatino

CONTENTS

TABLES AND FIGURES

PREFACE   This is the Center for Effective Organizations' (CEO) third study of the human resources (HR) function in large corporations. Like the previous studies, it is focused on measuring whether the HR function is changing and on gauging its effectiveness. The study focuses particularly on whether the HR function is changing to become more of a strategic business partner and whether it is becoming a value-added contributor to organizational performance. It also analyzes how organizations can more effectively manage their human capital. The present study focuses on many of the same corporations that we studied in 1995 and 1998. Thus, it allows us to compare data from our earlier studies to data we collected in 2001.

We are deeply indebted to the Human Resource Planning Society for its support of our research and all three of our studies. We would also like to thank the Marshall School of Business at the University of Southern California for its continuing support of the activities of CEO. In addition, we would like to thank the corporate sponsors of CEO for their support of the center and its mission; their support is vital to the overall success of the center and is directly responsible for enabling us to do the kind of research reported here.

We would also like to thank Dan Canning for his help in preparing the manuscript.

THE AUTHORS

Edward E. Lawler III joined the faculty of Yale University as assistant professor of industrial administration and psychology after receiving his Ph.D. from the University of California at Berkeley in 1964. Three years later, he was promoted to associate professor.

Lawler moved to the University of Michigan in 1972 as a professor of psychology and also became program director in the Survey Research Center at the Institute for Social Research. He held a Fulbright fellowship at the London Graduate School of Business. In 1978, he became a professor in the Marshall School of Business at the University of Southern California. During 1979, he founded and became director of the university's Center for Effective Organizations. In 1982, he was named professor of research at the University of Southern California. In 1999, he was named distinguished professor.

Ed Lawler has been honored as a major contributor to theory, research, and practice in the fields of human resources management, compensation, organizational development, and organizational effectiveness. He is the author and coauthor of over two hundred articles and thirty-five books. His most recent books include *From the Ground Up: Six Principles for Creating the New Logic Corporation* (Jossey-Bass, 1996); *Tomorrow's Organization* (Jossey-Bass, 1998); *The Leadership Change Handbook* (Jossey-Bass, 1999); *Rewarding Excellence* (Jossey-Bass, 2000); *Corporate Boards: New Strategies for Adding Value at the Top* (Jossey-Bass, 2001); and *Organizing for High Performance* (Jossey-Bass, 2001). His most recent book is *Treat People Right* (Jossey-Bass, 2003).

Susan Albers Mohrman is a senior research scientist at the Center for Effective Organizations in the Marshall School of Business at the University of Southern California. She received her B.A. in psychology from Stanford University and her Ph.D in organizational behavior from Northwestern University.

She has published papers in professional journals and books on the topics of building the knowledge organization; the design of organizations; organization development, learning, and change; high technology organizations; the design of teams and other lateral approaches to organizing; the human resource organization; and innovative research and evaluation methodologies. She is an editor of *Research for Theory and Practice* (Lexington Press, 1999); *Large-Scale Organizational Change* (Jossey-Bass, 1989); and *Managing Complexity in High Technology*

Organizations (Oxford University Press, 1989). She is coauthor of *Self-Designing Organizations: Learning How to Create High Performance* (Addison-Wesley, 1989); *School-Based Management: Learning to Create High Performance* (Jossey-Bass, 1994); *Designing Team-Based Organizations* (Jossey-Bass, 1995); *Strategies for High-Performance Organizations* (Jossey-Bass, 1998 and 2001); and *Tomorrow's Organization: Crafting Winning Capabilities in a Dynamic World* (Jossey-Bass, 1998).

Dr. Mohrman has done research for and consulted to a wide variety of organizations, in many different sectors of the economy, toward redesigning their structures and systems to create high performance.

The Authors

INTRODUCTION Global competition, information technology (IT), new knowledge, the growth of knowledge workers, and a host of other business environment changes are forcing organizations to constantly evaluate how they operate. In many cases, organizations are embracing new strategic initiatives and fundamentally changing how they operate. They are using new technologies, changing their structures, and improving work processes to respond to an increasingly demanding and global customer base. These initiatives entail fundamental change that has significant implications for the human resources and the HR function of organizations.

It is obvious that HR management practices should be an important part of the strategy of any large corporation. The annual reports of many corporations argue that their human capital and intellectual property are their most important assets. In addition, in many organizations, compensation is one of the largest costs, if not the largest. In service organizations, compensation often represents 70 to 80 percent of the total cost of doing business. With training costs and other HR management costs added to compensation costs, the HR function often has responsibilities that affect a large portion of an organization's total expenditures.

But the cost of HR is not the only or even the most important consideration for many organizations. Even when HR accounts for very little of the cost of doing business, it can have a significant impact on the organization's performance. In essence, without effective human resources, organizations are likely to have little or no revenue. Even the most automated production facilities require skilled, motivated employees to operate. Knowledge work organizations depend on employees to develop, use, and manage their most important asset, knowledge. Thus, although a company's human capital does not appear on its balance sheet, it represents an increasingly large percent of many organizations' market valuation (Lev, 2001).

Present Role of the HR Organization

Despite compelling arguments supporting HR management as a key strategic issue in most organizations, HR executives often are not strategic partners (Lawler, 1995; Brockbank, 1999). Instead, the HR function is largely an administrative function headed by individuals whose roles are focused on cost control and administrative activities (Ulrich, 1997).

One study of large corporations and another study that focused on a cross section of firms found that the major focus of most HR functions is on controlling costs and on a host of administrative issues (Lawler, Cohen, and Chang, 1993; BNA, 1994). Missing almost entirely from the list of HR focuses were key organizational challenges such as improving productivity, increasing quality, facilitating mergers and acquisitions, managing knowledge, and improving the ability of organizations to bring new products to market. Because the organizations likely saw these areas as important, we must ask why they were not the most important areas for the HR executives. Most likely, the executives in these firms simply felt that the HR function could not have an impact in these areas.

Studies provide some evidence that the situation is changing and that the HR function is beginning to redefine its role. One study found that 64 percent of the companies examined were transforming their HR organization (Csoka and Hackett, 1998). Our two previous studies found some change but noted that companies may be discussing change more than actually changing (Mohrman, Lawler, and McMahan, 1996; Lawler and Mohrman, 2000).

During the 1990s, a number of studies focused on the HR function (for example, the Conference Board study by Csoka and Hackett, 1998; the Human Resource Planning Society study by Eichinger and Ulrich, 1995, and one by Wright, Dyer, and Takla, 1999; the American Productivity and Quality Center study by Smith and Riley, 1994; studies by Becker and Huselid, 1998, 1999; Michigan studies by Ulrich, Brockbank, Yeung, and Lake, 1995). Among other issues, they focused on the competencies of the HR function and its executives, change efforts to revitalize the role of HR in initiatives such as Total Quality Management, and HR services and programs that will position the HR function acting as a business partner.

An interesting view of the HR function of the future is presented in the Corporate Leadership Council's book *Vision of the Future* (1995). It projects a gutting of the HR function as we know it today as many HR functions are transferred to the line, outside vendors, and high-efficiency processing centers. The HR function is expected to focus almost exclusively on business consulting and the management of the organization's core competencies. Ulrich (1997; Ulrich, Losey, and Lake, 1997) has further developed the argument that the HR function needs to be redesigned to operate as a business partner. He has also argued that organizations should develop a balanced scorecard for their HR function (Becker, Huselid, and Ulrich, 2001). Brockbank (1999) has argued that the HR function needs to become strategically proactive.

Describing the new HR role and defining the new competencies it needs are only the first steps in easing its transition to becoming a strategic business partner. For decades, the HR function has been organized to carry out an administrative function. Changing that role will require a different mix of activities and necessitate reconfiguring the HR function to support changing business strategies and organization designs (Mohrman and Lawler, 1993). It also will require the employees in the HR function to have very different competencies than they traditionally have had (Ulrich, Brockbank, Yeung, and Lake, 1995).

It is becoming increasingly clear that IT will play a very important role in the future of the HR function (Wright and Dyer, 2000). Many of HR's administrative tasks can be done by employees and managers on a self-service basis when companies use eHR systems. The intranet-based systems that currently exist can handle HR activities such as salary administration, job posting and placement, address changes, family changes, and benefits administration—in short, virtually every administrative function that the staff of an HR function typically does. In addition, these systems are available around the clock and can be accessed from virtually anywhere.

Perhaps the greatest value of eHR systems will result from their ability to integrate and analyze organizations' HR activities. They have the potential to make HR information much more accessible so that executives can use it to guide strategy development and implementation. eHR systems also can be used to more effectively develop and allocate the human capital of organizations.

Forces for Change: Strategic Change and the Value-Added Organization

The forces of global competition have sent shock waves that have left very few organizations untouched (Lawler, Mohrman, and Benson, 2001). Survival in today's world demands that organizations develop the capabilities to compete on many fronts: speed, cost, quality, service, technology, innovation, knowledge management, and new products, to name a few. Increasingly, the only sustainable competitive advantage is the ability to organize effectively, respond to change, and manage well (Mohrman, Galbraith, and Lawler, 1998). Lawler, Mohrman, and Benson's study (2001) of the Fortune 1000 provides confirmation of this, showing a significant relationship between the adoption of new management practices designed to increase the firm's capabilities and its financial performance.

A growing body of evidence indicates that HR can be a value-added function in organizations. The most important work on the relationship between firm performance and HR practices has been conducted by Becker and Huselid (1998). In their study of 740 corporations, they found that firms with the greatest intensity of HR practices that reinforce performance had the highest market value per employee. They go on to argue that HR practices are critical in determining the market value of a corporation and that improvements in HR practices can lead to significant increases in the market value of corporations. They conclude that the best firms are able to achieve both operational and strategic excellence in their HR systems.

Staff functions in general, and HR functions in particular, are under fire in organizations because they are frequently perceived as controlling rather than adding value and as not responding to the demands for change that come from operating units. Staff functions are being asked to provide expert support to the strategic initiatives of the company and to take advantage of technology and other approaches to deliver more efficient and responsive services.

Organizational design is increasingly being recognized as a key factor that enables organizations to develop capabilities and therefore to perform in ways that produce a competitive advantage. Organizations are adopting design features with an eye to the value they contribute, that is, how they help the organization accomplish its mission effectively (Galbraith, 2002). All parts of the organization, operating units and staff functions alike, are being redesigned to deliver higher value. For staff groups, this requires developing a *business model* that defines what kind of value the staff will deliver. It needs to make clear both how it will enhance company performance and why the company should pay for it. It then requires an organizational design for the support function that fits with that business model.

Researchers have noted two important trends in organizational design (Mohrman, Galbraith, and Lawler, 1998). First, design is being recognized as more than structure; it includes elements such as management processes, rewards, people systems, information systems, and work processes. These elements must fit with the strategy and with one another for an organization to perform effectively (Waterman, 1982; Nadler, Gerstein, and Shaw, 1992).

The HR organization must think about whether the elements of its design create a high-performance HR system, one capable of delivering maximum value while consuming the least possible resources. This means concentrating on the way it organizes to deliver routine transactional services, traditional HR systems development and administration, and strategic business support. The HR staff must think about HR's own structure, customer linkages, competency development, management processes, rewards, and use of IT to ensure that they optimally deploy their scarce resources to deliver value. In addition to making sure the HR function is optimally designed, HR may also add value by helping design the total organization and its business units.

Second, organizational designs are being acknowledged to involve complex trade-offs and contingencies, and that as a result one design does not fit all organizations. New business models are emerging, and many new approaches and organizational forms are springing up to deal with the complex requirements that organizations must address (Mohrman, Galbraith, and Lawler, 1998). These include complex partnerships, globally integrated firms, customer-focused designs, and network organizations. Furthermore, multibusiness corporations are recognizing that different businesses exist in different markets and face varying requirements. Consequently, there is increasing variation in organizational design within multibusiness corporations and between businesses (Galbraith, 2002). This means that one type of HR function does not fit all situations. Different organizational forms require different kinds of HR contributions and thus different HR designs and systems.

Designing the HR Function

Organizational design decisions must be made in four key areas for the HR function as well as for organizations as a whole:

- Which functions should be centralized and leveraged, and which should be decentralized in order to provide focus on the unique needs of different parts of the organization? Organizations are combining centralization and decentralization: trying to be big (coordinated) in functions such as purchasing when there is an advantage to being big and trying to be small (decentralized and flexible) in functions such as new product development when there are advantages to being small and agile.

- Which functions should be performed in-house and which should be outsourced? Companies are outsourcing when they can purchase high-quality services and products more inexpensively or reliably than they can generate them internally (Arthur Andersen and Economist Intelligence Unit, 1995).

- Which functions should be hierarchically controlled, and which should be integrated and controlled laterally? In some areas, organizations function best laterally, integrating and creating synergies across various parts of the organization, creating cross-functional units to carry out entire processes, and collaborating with suppliers and customers (Mohrman, Cohen, and Mohrman, 1995). Organizations are searching for ways to leverage across business units while setting up organizational and management approaches to allow the optimal levels of flexibility and control to various business units.

- Which processes should be IT based? Many organizations have gone through process reengineering (Hammer and Champy, 1993) to redesign and simplify processes, eliminate processes that do not add value, and take maximum advantage of automation capabilities. They are rapidly adopting enterprise resource planning (ERP), Web-based, and e-commerce IT to speed up their operations, reduce costs, and better integrate their activities.

Traditionally, HR and many other staff groups such as IT have been organized hierarchically and have seen their mission as designing, administering, and enforcing adherence to HR policies and systems. They have been seen as expensive: a necessary evil consuming resources disproportionate to the value that they add to the company. Among the changes in structure and process that are being advocated for staff functions such as HR are the following (Lawler and Galbraith, 1993; Mohrman, Galbraith, Lawler, and Associates, 1998):

- Decentralizing business support to operating units in order to increase responsiveness

- Contracting with business units for the services that will be delivered and perhaps even requiring services to be self-funding as a way of ensuring that businesses get only the services they are willing to pay for and that they see as contributing to business performance

- Finding the most efficient way to deliver processing and transactional services, such as creating efficient central services and/or contracting out centralized processing units

- Using IT to make processes more efficient and/or to deliver increased value

- Participating in cross-unit teams in order to deliver integrated services, partner with customers to increase line ownership over HR systems, and bring the HR perspective to cross-functional team activities

- Creating shared centers of excellence that provide expert services often in a consulting capacity to the businesses

- Increasing the rotation of people within various staff functions and between staff and line, making for fewer lifelong careers within a narrow staff function, in order to broaden the perspectives of HR staff professionals and their awareness of business issues, as well as to increase depth of understanding of HR issues among line management

Future Role of the HR Organization

The future of the HR function in organizations is very uncertain. On the one hand, if current trends continue, it could end up being largely an administrative function that manages an IT-based HR system. Alternatively, it could become a driver of organizational effectiveness and business strategy. This opportunity exists now because many of the key determinants of competitive advantage depend on effective human capital management (Jackson, Hitt, and DeNisi, 2003). More than ever before, the effectiveness of organizations depends on their ability to address issues such as knowledge management, change management, and capability building, all of which could fall into the domain of the HR function. The unanswered question at this point is whether they will rise to the occasion.

In order to increase their contribution to organizational effectiveness in the future, HR professionals must rethink their function's structure, services, and programs to address how it can add value in today's economy with its new organizational forms and business strategies. HR faces a formidable challenge just in helping organizations deal with the human issues that are raised by large-scale strategic change. To face these challenges effectively, HR has to focus on how it can add value and how it is organized; it must improve its competencies and in some areas develop new ones.

A number of studies have addressed the new competencies required as the HR function strives to be a business partner in this changing environment (for example, Smith and Riley, 1994; Csoka, 1995; Eichinger and Ulrich, 1995; Ulrich, 1997; Csoka and Hackett, 1998) and to align with the business. Identifying these competencies is only the first step. It needs to be followed by organizing the HR function to develop these competencies and to provide services in a manner that adds value as organizations change their overall architecture and strategy.

To develop, the HR function must get out of the control and audit role and take on a management and development role. Lawler (1995) develops this line of thought further by arguing that the HR management approach (Figure I-1) does not go far enough in meeting business needs. He argues that the HR function should take a business partner approach (Figure I-2).

The business partner approach emphasizes that the role of the HR function involves developing systems and practices to ensure that the company's employees have the needed competencies and are motivated to perform effectively. HR has a seat at the table when business issues are discussed, and it brings an HR perspective to these discussions. When it comes to designing HR systems and practices, the line organization is involved in the process so that they own the systems. HR relies on the line to effectively implement many of the HR practices; HR measures the effectiveness of these practices and focuses on process improvements.

The business partner approach clearly positions the HR function as a value-added part of an organization. In this approach, the HR function contributes to business performance by effectively managing the most important capital of most organizations, their human capital. But even

AIMS	Business orientation.
	Services provided expressed as outputs or products.
	Voice of the customer.
PROCESS	Build performance-management capabilities.
	Develop managers: link competencies to job requirements and career development.
	Plan for succession.
	Enhance organizational change capabilities.
	Build an organizationwide HR network.
PLANNING	HR (and all other functions) inspect business plans; inputs from HR may be inserted in the planning process.

Source: Based on Evans (1994).

Figure I-1. HR Management

AIMS	Line management owns human resources as a part of its role.
	HR is an integral member of management teams.
	Culture of the firm evolves to fit with strategy and vision.
PROCESS	Organize HR flexibly around the work to be done (programs and projects, outsourcing).
	Focus on the development of people and organizations (road maps, teams, organizational design).
	Leverage competencies, manage learning linkages; build organizational work redesign capabilities.
	Develop leadership.
PLANNING	An integral component of strategic and business planning by the management team.

Source: Based on Evans (1994).

Figure I-2. Business Partner

this may not be the approach that leads to the HR function adding the most value it can. By becoming a strategic partner (see Figure I-3), the potential exists for the HR function to add more value.

When HR is a strategic partner, its role includes helping the organization develop its strategy, as well as transform and develop itself. In the knowledge economy, a firm's strategy is closely linked to its human tal-

Introduction

AIMS	HR is a major influence on business strategy.
	HR systems drive business performance.
PROCESS	Self-service for transactional work.
	Transactional work outsourced.
	Knowledge management.
	Focus on organization development.
	Change management.
	Human resource processes tied to business strategies.
PLANNING	HR is a key contributor to strategic planning and change management.

Figure I-3. Strategic Partner

ent. An HR function that is positioned and designed as a strategic partner participates in both strategy formulation and implementation because expertise in attracting, retaining, developing, deploying, and motivating human capital is critical to both. Ideally, the HR function is knowledgeable about the business and expert in organizational and work design issues, so it can help the company develop needed organizational capabilities and change rapidly as new opportunities become available.

In order for HR to be a strategic partner, HR executives need an expert understanding of business strategy, organizational design, change management, and the integration of HR practices and strategies to support organizational designs and strategies. They need to bring to the table a perspective that is often missing in discussions of business strategy and change: knowledge about the human capital factors and organizational change that are critical in determining whether a strategy can be implemented. This is a particularly important perspective given that many more strategies fail because of implementation problems rather than conceptual flaws.

Focus of Study

There has been a great deal of rhetoric about change in the HR function. A recent report from the Human Resource Planning Society (Wright, Dyer, and Takla, 1999) makes the point that a consensus now exists about what the HR organization should become but that the function has been slow to develop the capabilities to execute that vision. The overarching focus of this study is on how HR organizations are changing in response to the strategic and organizational initiatives that businesses are undertaking. The present study examines the extent to which the design and activities of the HR function are actually changing by comparing data from 1995, 1998, and 2001. We examine the prevalence of the practices that we earlier said represent the new directions that HR organizations should take to fit with the strategic changes that are occurring in the broader organizations they serve. We also examine whether these changes are uniform across organizations and whether they characterize some kinds of companies more than others. Finally, we examine the impact of changes in the HR function on its effectiveness, as seen from within the function. This gives us a sense of the developing business models and belief system within the HR function about what constitutes effective HR practice (its value proposition), whether fully in place or not.

This study focuses in depth on eight areas:

1. *The HR Role and Activities.* Because of change in the business environment, it is reasonable to expect that the HR function may have changed the amount of emphasis it places on a variety of HR roles and activities. A major focus of this study is on how much the HR function is becoming a strategic partner and on what organization designs and HR practices are associated with this. Of particular concern is whether increased attention to strategic services, such as organization design and development, affect the perceived effectiveness of the HR function. The study will also focus on measuring how much change has occurred in the emphasis on traditional HR functions such as HR planning, compensation, recruitment, selection, and benefits administration.

2. *The Design of the HR Function.* We will examine whether changes have occurred in the way the HR function is organized in order to increase the value that it delivers.

3. *Shared Services Units.* Because of its linchpin role in the balance between efficiency and leverage and customer-focused support, we focus extensively on the adoption of shared services and centers of excellence. Companies create these units in order to gain economies of scale and improve expertise. These approaches may be particularly effective when a company has multiple business units; it can gain economies of scale and has the potential to gain in expertise by having parts of the HR function that serve the entire corporation. Key issues that we study involve what functions are best put into shared services units and, of course, how effective the shared services units are.

4. *Outsourcing.* Another increasingly popular way to deliver HR services and gain HR expertise is outsourcing. It is one way to deal with changes in the demand for HR services as well as a way to control costs. Thus, this study focuses both on how common outsourcing is

and the problems that it produces. Clearly, managing contractors is sometimes difficult; thus, it is also important to know how effectively HR deals with vendors.

5. *IT.* eHR has the potential to radically change the way HR services are delivered and managed. Thus, the present study examines how companies are using IT in their HR functions. It looks in detail at how computer systems are being used and at how effective they are with respect to such activities as salary planning, performance management, and new-hire orientation. It also focuses on how eHR systems are developed and how effective organizations consider their eHR systems to be in positively influencing employee satisfaction and loyalty, business effectiveness, and the analysis of strategic information.

6. *Talent Strategy.* Numerous books and articles have highlighted the fact that organizations are increasingly competing for human capital. They also, of course, need to effectively manage the talent. The present study focuses on the approaches that are involved in company's talent strategies. One particular focus is on whether organizations have singled out employees with high potential and whether they get special treatment.

7. *HR Skills.* A critical issue in the effectiveness of any HR function is the skills of the HR professionals and staff. Thus, the present study asks about how satisfied organizations are with their HR professionals' skills in a variety of areas. It particularly focuses on those skills that HR professionals need in order to serve as true business and strategic partners.

8. *HR Effectiveness.* The effectiveness of the HR function in a number of areas is a critical issue. Thus, any study of the HR function needs to gather data about how effectively the HR function is currently performing. Particular emphasis in the present study is on the HR function's effectiveness in doing many of the new activities that are required in order for HR to be a business and strategic partner. These include managing change, contributing to strategy, managing the outsourcing of HR, and operating shared services units. Perhaps the crucial issue with respect to effectiveness concerns what practices lead to an effective HR organization. Thus, the present study will determine what HR structures, approaches, and practices are associated with the effectiveness of the HR organization.

Overall, the focus of the present study is on how the HR function is changing in response to changes in the business environment. We are uniquely able to look at and measure the degree of change because of the longitudinal nature of the study.

THE STUDY AND SAMPLE

This is the third study in a series examining whether changes in the HR organizations of large corporations are taking place. The first study was done in 1995 and covered 417 large and medium-sized service and industrial firms (Mohrman, Lawler, and McMahan, 1996). The second study was done in 1998 and covered 663 similar firms (Lawler and Mohrman, 2000). The present survey was done in 2001 and was mailed to 966 HR managers who were in director or above positions, with corporatewide visibility of the HR function. It was mailed to large and medium-sized corporations that were either sponsors of the Center for Effective Organizations or members of the Human Resource Planning Society.

This study, like the 1995 and 1998 studies, used a three-step data collection procedure. First, we mailed out surveys. Second, four weeks after the initial mailing, we mailed reminder letters to all firms that had not returned completed surveys. Third, sixty days later, we sent a second questionnaire to firms that had not yet responded.

For the 2001 study, we received 150 usable questionnaires, a response rate of 15.5 percent. In 1998, we received 119 usable surveys, a response rate of 17.9 percent. In 1995, we had a sample of 130 companies, a response rate of 19.6 percent.

The 2001 surveys were generally filled out by individuals in large companies from a variety of industries. This was also true of our 1995 and 1998 surveys. The average organizational size in 1998 was 34,948, which was almost identical to the number in 1995. In 2001, the average size was 21,000. Therefore, readers should consider our findings as characterizing large companies.

The smaller size of companies in the 2001 sample seems to be due to several factors. First, 2001 was a time of layoffs and downsizing, so many companies were smaller than they had been in the boom times of 1995 and 1998. Further, several of the very large firms that participated in the 1995 and 1998 surveys did not participate in the 2001 survey.

The difference in company size raises the question of whether any differences between the 2001 and the earlier surveys might be due to changes in the nature of the sample. In order to check this, we did all of our analyses on both the total sample for 2001 and on only those companies that responded to both the 1998 and 2001 surveys. Based on this analysis, it appears that the changes we found from 1998 to 2001 are not due to differences in the size of the companies in the two samples.

Measures

The 2001 survey was an expanded version of the two previous surveys. It covered eleven areas:

1. General descriptive information about the demographics of the firm and the HR function

2. The organizational context that the HR function serves, including its broad organizational form and the amount and kinds of strategic change and organizational initiatives that the company is carrying out

3. The changing focus of the HR function measured in terms of how much time it is spending in different kinds of roles compared with five to seven years ago

4. The extent of emphasis that a number of HR activities are receiving

5. Talent strategies (new in 2001)

6. HR's use of various organizational practices to increase efficiency and business responsiveness and the extent to which HR is investing in a number of strategic initiatives to support strategic change

7. The use of shared services units and their effectiveness (new in 1998)

8. The use of outsourcing and the problems that have been encountered (new in 1998)

9. The use of IT and its effectiveness (new in 1998, expanded in 2001)

10. The changing skill requirements for employees in the HR function and satisfaction with current skills

11. The perceived effectiveness of the HR function

The findings will be reported in roughly this order. (A complete copy of the 2001 survey with frequencies, means, and variances for each item appears in the Appendix.)

Staffing of HR Function

In the firms studied, the average number of employees in the HR function was 234; this represents a significant decrease from 1998, when the number was 402, and from the 1995 number of 377. The smaller size of the HR function undoubtedly is due to the smaller size of the companies in 2001. The ratio of HR employees to the total number of employees was 90:1 in 2001. Little changed from the ratio of 87:1 in 1998 and 92:1 in 1995.

The ratio of HR staffing in this study is generally in line with ratios found in other studies. For example, the 2000–2001 BNA survey reports

Table S-1. HR Generalists and Specialists			
Percentage of HR Employees	**1995**	**1998**	**2001**
HR generalist	46	46	43
Corporate staff	44	43	46

a ratio of 100:1 (BNA, 2001). This is essentially the same ratio reported in its 1997 survey (BNA, 2001). Thus, there is no evidence that the HR function is decreasing in size relative to the rest of the organization. Why this is true is unclear. It may reflect the importance of the function or simply that the function is a well-institutionalized part of most organizations that is difficult to reduce in size.

Demographic information on staffing of the HR function for the firms in the 1995, 1998, and 2001 studies is portrayed in Table S-1. Of the professional-managerial HR staff in 2001, 43 percent were described as generalists. The percentage of the HR professional-managerial staff that are part of a centralized corporate staff function is 46 percent. Overall, there has been no significant change in the staffing of HR functions from 1995 to 2001.

Companies in the 2001 sample typically operated in several countries; 63.3 percent had more than 5 percent of their revenue come from outside the United States. In the companies that operated internationally, only 17 percent of HR professionals were located outside the United States, whereas 25.7 percent of their employees were outside the United States. This suggests that there may be less staffing of the HR function outside of the United States than inside the United States; undoubtedly, this is because to some degree corporate services from the United States are provided to employees in other countries.

The respondents were asked to state the background of the current head of HR. In 75 percent of cases, the top HR executive came up through the HR function. In the other 25 percent of cases, these executives came from functions such as operations, sales and marketing, and legal.

The percentage of HR executives in 2001 who did not have a background in HR is slightly higher than the 21 percent we found in 1995. A number of firms clearly are continuing to put executives in charge of the HR function who are not career HR employees. Why is this happening? We can suggest three likely reasons. The first is to develop senior executives without an HR background because they are candidates for

The Study and Sample

the job of chief executive officer. Second, they are being put in charge in order to make HR run more like a business and be more of a business partner. Third, failed line managers are being put into HR because it is a safe preretirement job. The survey did not ask why this is being done, so we can only speculate. That said, we think in the majority of cases it is done in order to change the HR function or to develop an executive. In today's business world, the job of HR executive is too important a position to use as a dumping ground.

Organizational Forms

Most organizations start out as simple structures that offer a small number of products and services and serve a defined market. They have small staff groups and are organized based on functions such as sales and manufacturing. They are often small enough to operate largely through informal coordination. As organizations grow and the number of products, services, and markets increases, informal coordination is no longer adequate. The structure grows in complexity and formality as the organization goes through phases of growth. If the company relies on one major set of technologies and a set of related products that can be developed, marketed, and distributed in similar ways, the company may retain a functional form (Mohrman, Galbraith, and Lawler, 1998). When this happens, a centralized HR function typically provides services to the organization.

If the company grows through increasing its variety of products and services and the diversity of its markets and distribution channels, it may divide into multiple business units, each of which is a complete multifunctional structure. As long as these business units are related, perhaps because they rely on common technology, serve similar customers, or distribute through a common channel, companies usually have a centralized HR function. Here, the HR challenge is to organize the function to allow businesses to pursue their unique needs and strategies while providing economies of scale and a foundation for integration across the businesses where it is desirable.

When a company diversifies to the extent that it houses a number of quite different businesses that have different markets, technologies, and distribution channels, it usually is organized into groups or sectors, each of which houses a number of related businesses. When this occurs, the opportunities for synergy among groups are limited. Nevertheless, the corporation may continue to add value by carrying out some activities, such as HR, on a corporationwide basis. Alternatively, a company may choose to manage its businesses as a financial portfolio only and may adopt a holding company form that has little or no corporate staff. In this approach, each business unit has its own HR staff.

Table S-2. Organizational Structure					
	Single Integrated Business	Multiple Related Business	Several-Sector Businesses	Multiple Unrelated Businesses	Large Companies
2001 Percentages	25.7	38.5	26.4	5.4	32.0
1998 Percentages	23.5	49.6	26.1	0	47.9
1995 Percentages	29.1	40.9	26.0	1.6	44.5

Table S-2 shows the breakdown of the companies in our 1995, 1998, and 2001 studies on the basis of their structure. By far the largest group of companies in all of the studies are those with multiple related business units. Single integrated businesses and corporations with multiple sectors or groups of businesses compose most of the remainder. There are also a few corporations that are composed of multiple unrelated businesses. Unfortunately, because of the small number of these firms, we cannot analyze our data in order to determine if they differ from the other types.

Table S-2 also shows the percentage of companies that are large, that is, with more than twenty thousand employees. Organizational size is important to consider because it often influences how corporate staff groups, such as HR, are structured and operated.

All the structural types of organization that are represented in our studies face common decisions about how to organize HR and other support functions. They must decide how much commonality and integration of practice they want across business units and how much they want to organize to achieve economies of scale. These objectives have to be weighed against the objectives of delivering services that are tailored for each part of the organization and that are delivered in a manner that supports flexibility and optimization at the level of the business unit.

The configuration of businesses in the corporate portfolio is particularly important in determining how staff functions such as HR are organized and positioned. The shape of a staff group, such as HR, that results from an analysis of how it should be positioned may differ depending on the structure of the organization. The design for an integrated business, in which HR does not have to support varied business strategies, is likely to differ from that in a multiple-business corporation, in which different businesses may require different HR approaches. The integrated business may reduce costs by creating corporate HR shared services groups.

The multiple-business corporation may optimize value by creating economies of scale through centrally servicing areas that do not require business-specific adaptation. It may also optimize value by decentralizing or outsourcing the provision of service that has to be tailored to particular operating units. Because of the potential effects of structure on the HR function, we will analyze our data to see how organization structure relates to the design and operation of the HR function.

The Strategic and Organizational Context

HR organizations exist in organizational environments that are as turbulent as the competitive environments in which companies find themselves. As companies take measures to survive and prosper, they make changes and introduce initiatives that change the organization, the competencies it has, the way it manages its human resources, and its expectations of and relationships with its employees (Lawler, 1996; Lawler, Mohrman, and Ledford, 1998). Thus, in order to understand the HR function of an organization, we must examine how its characteristics are related to the organization's strategic focuses and change initiatives.

Table S-3 shows the prevalence of a number of strategic focuses that are often part of a company's business strategy. It also shows that the items measuring strategic focus divide into four groups: growth, knowledge- and information-based strategies, core business focus, and quality and speed. The items concerned with knowledge and information and quality and speed received the highest ratings. The customer focus item was rated the highest, and it also showed the largest increase from 1995.

The survey also asked about the use of specific change initiatives and activities that companies frequently use to implement business strategies. As Table S-4 indicates, when analyzed statistically, the items measuring organizational change initiatives fell into three groups: restructuring, organizational performance, and competency and knowledge management. The restructuring items received the highest ratings, particularly the item of cost containment.

A comparison of the 1995, 1998, and 2001 results shows two interesting trends. Downsizing and reducing layers have decreased in importance as has Total Quality Management. This finding is consistent with other research that shows a decrease in the focus on quality programs (Lawler, Mohrman, and Benson, 2001). Much to our surprise, given the economy in 2001, we found that downsizing, reducing layers, and cost containment decreased. In addition to quality, a decrease in the focus on teams and employee involvement is apparent. These may be victims of the poor economy that existed in 2001. Given that no change initiatives

Table S-3. Strategic Focuses			
	Means		
	1995	**1998**	**2001**
Growth	—	**3.2**	**2.9**
Building a global presence	3.4	3.2	3.0
Acquisitions	2.8	3.5	3.1*
Entering new businesses	—	2.8	2.6
Core Business	—	**2.4**	**2.5**
Partnering/networking with other companies	2.9	2.8	3.1
Reducing the number of businesses you are in	—	1.9	1.9
Quality and Speed	**3.7**	**3.5**	**3.7**
Cycle time reduction	3.5	3.4	3.4
Accelerating new product innovation	3.7	3.5	3.7
Quality	3.9	3.6	3.9*
Knowledge- and Information-Based Strategies	—	—	**3.7**
Process automation/IT	4.1	3.9	3.8
Customer focus	3.4	4.4	4.4*
Technology leadership	3.9	3.6	3.5*
Talent—being an employer of choice	—	—	3.8
e-Business	—	—	3.2

Response scale: 1 = little or no extent; 2 = some extent; 3 = moderate extent; 4 = great extent; 5 = very great extent.

Note: Items with (—) were not asked.

* = Significant difference at $p \leq .05$ (one-way analysis of variance).

increased from 1998 to 2001, it seems most likely that most companies decreased the spending on these initiatives in the face of a poor economy.

The changes shown in Tables S-3 and S-4 are a strong statement of why an organization's HR function has to be prepared to make changes in its systems. Downsizing and total quality programs require supportive HR systems and practices that may not be a good fit in an organization that is focusing on other change initiatives. They also have implications for how the HR function should be structured and managed.

The prevalence of the four strategic focuses in the different organizational forms is shown in Table S-5. Respondents most frequently report quality and speed and knowledge- and information-based strategies as the strategic focus in all types of organizations. There are no significant differences in strategic focus among the three organizational types.

Table S-6 shows the prevalence of the organizational change initiatives in the different organizational forms. Of these three change initiatives, restructuring initiatives are the most prevalent in all types of organiza-

Table S-4. Change Initiatives

	Means		
	1995	**1998**	**2001**
Restructuring	—	**3.5**	**3.3**
Restructuring	4.1	4.0	4.0
Downsizing	3.6	3.1	2.9*
Reducing layers/flattening	3.4	3.3	3.0*
Outsourcing	2.8	2.9	2.8
Cost containment	—	4.3	4.0
Organizational Performance	**3.3**	**3.2**	**3.0***
Reengineering	3.4	3.2	3.1
Team structures	3.3	3.2	2.8*
Process management	3.3	3.2	3.2
Total Quality Management/Six Sigma	3.4	2.8	2.5*
Employee involvement	3.4	3.5	3.2*
Competency and Knowledge Management	—	**2.9**	**3.0**
Knowledge/intellectual capital management	—	2.9	2.9
Employee competency management	—	3.0	3.0

Response scale: 1 = little or no extent; 2 = some extent; 3 = moderate extent; 4 = great extent; 5 = very great extent.

* = Significant difference at $p \leq .05$ (one-way analysis of variance).

Table S-5. Strategic Focuses

	All Companies		Single Integrated Business		Multiple Related Business		Several Business Sectors	
Strategic Focuses	**1998**	**2001**	**1998**	**2001**	**1998**	**2001**	**1998**	**2001**
Growth	3.2	2.9	2.8	2.6	3.2	2.9	3.3	3.1
Core business	2.4	2.5	2.1	2.4	2.3	2.5	2.7	2.5
Quality and speed	3.5	3.7	3.5	3.6	3.4	3.7	3.7	3.6
Knowledge- and information-based strategies	—	3.7	—	3.6	—	3.8	—	3.7

Means; response scale: 1 = little or no extent; 2 = some extent; 3 = moderate extent; 4 = great extent; 5 = very great extent.

tions. We found no significant difference in the application of these organizational performance approaches among single integrated, multiple related, and multiple-group or -sector companies. The single integrated business organizations tended to focus less on restructuring in both 1998 and 2001.

Table S-6. Change Initiatives								
	All Companies		Single Integrated Business		Multiple Related Business		Several Business Sectors	
Change Initiatives	1998	2001	1998	2001	1998	2001	1998	2001
Restructuring	3.5	3.3	3.3	3.0	3.5	3.5	3.7	3.4
Organizational performance	3.2	3.0	3.0	2.8	3.2	3.0	3.3	2.9
Competency and knowledge management	2.9	3.0	3.0	3.0	2.9	3.0	3.0	3.0

Means; response scale: 1 = little or no extent; 2 = some extent; 3 = moderate extent; 4 = great extent; 5 = very great extent.

On balance, our data support the point that organizations exist in dynamic environments and have in place a variety of strategic and organizational initiatives to better position themselves to perform successfully. The HR function, if it is to add value and act as a strategic partner, needs to help ensure that the organizational capabilities and competencies exist to cope with a dynamic environment. Thus, the HR function needs to cope with a shifting terrain. In order to determine how it is coping, we will look not only at how the HR function is changing but also at how companies' strategies and their change initiatives are changing the HR function.

SECTION 1

Role of HR

Respondents were asked to estimate the percentage of time that the HR function currently spends carrying out a number of roles versus how much time it spent five to seven years ago. Table 1.1 shows that our respondents report a significant change. According to them, the HR staff is spending less time on record keeping and auditing functions and more time on developing new systems and practices and on being a strategic business partner. We found no significant change in providing services (helping with the implementation and administration of HR practices). Overall, our respondents report significant movement toward HR becoming a strategic partner and doing higher value-added activities. However, before we conclude that this has actually occurred, let's look at the results from 1995 and 1998.

The data from 1995 and 1998 are almost identical to the data we collected in 2001 for the same question (see Tables 1.2 and 1.3). This finding makes two interesting points. First, it means that between 1995 and 2001 there has not been much change in how HR executives see the HR function spending its time. Second, it raises serious questions about the validity of our respondents' reports about how things were five to seven years earlier. One might expect that the 2001 estimates of how things were five to seven years earlier would be somewhat in line with how respondents said things were in our 1995 study, but they are not. Instead, the 1995 results are the same as the results for 2001! This finding suggests that the HR executives who responded in 2001, as well as those who responded in 1995 and 1998, may have perceived more change in their role than has actually taken place.

What should we believe, retrospective reports of the way things were or data from the past about the way things were? The answer is obvious: individuals are much better at reporting how things are now than they are at reporting on how things were years ago. In short, they probably are guilty of a bit of wishful thinking when they compare their present situation to the past, because they want to see themselves as being more of a strategic partner now than they were in the recent past.

We found the same time allocation results for companies of all structures: single integrated businesses, multiple related businesses, and groups or sectors of businesses. We also found no relationship between organization size and time allocation. This is a bit surprising; we expected that strategic business partnering might be higher in companies that have multiple businesses because they often face complex HR

Compare w/p

Table 1.1. Percentage of Time Spent on Various HR Roles (2001)

	Means		
	5 to 7 Years Ago	Current	Difference
Maintaining Records Collect, track, and maintain data on employees	26.8	14.9	Significant decrease
Auditing/Controlling Ensure compliance to internal operations, regulations, and legal and union requirements	17.1	11.4	Significant decrease
HR Service Provider Assist with implementation and administration of HR practices	33.1	31.3	No significant change
Development of HR Systems and Practices Develop new HR systems and practices	13.9	19.3	Significant increase
Strategic Business Partner Member of the management team; involved with strategic HR planning, organizational design, and strategic change	9.1	23.2	Significant increase

Table 1.2. Percentage of Time Spent on Various HR Roles (1998)

	Means		
	5 to 7 Years Ago	Current	Difference
Maintaining Records Collect, track, and maintain data on employees	25.6	16.1	Significant decrease
Auditing/Controlling Ensure compliance to internal operations, regulations, and legal and union requirements	16.4	11.2	Significant decrease
HR Service Provider Assist with implementation and administration of HR practices	36.4	35.0	No significant change
Development of HR Systems and Practices Develop new HR systems and practices	14.2	19.2	Significant increase
Strategic Business Partner Member of the management team; involved with strategic HR planning, organizational design, and strategic change	9.4	20.3	Significant increase

Table 1.3. Percentage of Time Spent on Various HR Roles (1995)

	Means		
	5 to 7 Years Ago	Current	Difference
Maintaining Records Collect, track, and maintain data on employees	22.9	15.4	Significant decrease
Auditing/Controlling Ensure compliance to internal operations, regulations, and legal and union requirements	19.5	12.2	Significant decrease
HR Service Provider Assist with implementation and administration of HR practices	34.3	31.3	Significant decrease
Development of HR Systems and Practices Develop new HR systems and practices	14.3	18.6	Significant increase
Strategic Business Partner Member of the management team; involved with strategic HR planning, organizational design, and strategic change	10.3	21.9	Significant increase

Table 1.4. Relationship of Strategic Focuses and Change Initiatives to HR Roles

	Strategic Focuses				Change Initiatives		
	Growth	Core Business	Quality & Speed	Knowledge- & Information-Based Strategies	Restructuring	Organizational Performance	Competency & Knowledge Management
Maintaining records	-.10	-.04	-.02	.01	-.10	.11	-.05
Auditing/controlling	.00	-.02	.14	.01	.14	.09	-.12
Providing HR services	-.08	-.04	-.23**	-.09	-.13	-.13	-.22**
Developing HR systems	.03	-.06	-.13	-.15	.13	-.18*	-.01
Strategic business partnering	.12	.10	.26***	.15	.05	.13	.31***

Zero order correlation: * $p \leq 0.05$; ** $p \leq 0.01$; *** $p \leq 0.001$.

issues involving how the corporate staff and business units relate to each other.

The results concerning the relationship of strategic focuses and change initiatives to the HR role are shown in Table 1.4. Business strategies focusing on quality and speed are negatively related to providing services and positively related to strategic business partnering. This result is not surprising because achieving quality and speed requires supportive HR systems and strategies and a focus on nontraditional HR issues such as work and organization design. We might expect that knowledge strategies would be related to strategic business partnering, but this relationship does not quite reach statistical significance.

The results concerning the relationship between the change initiatives and the HR role show three significant relationships. As we might expect, the more an organization tries to build competency and knowledge management capabilities, the more focus the HR organization has on business partnering. Spending time on providing services shows a negative relationship to employee competency and knowledge management, indicating that when knowledge management is the focus, HR spends less time on services and more time on business partnering. This follows directly from the fact that effective competency and knowledge management are dependent on successfully positioning an organization's human resources relative to its business strategy. Hence, it also follows that the HR organization would be more involved in business

Table 1.5. HR's Role in Strategy

(Means are of percentages)	All Companies		Single Integrated Business	Multiple Related Business	Several-Sector Businesses	Large Companies
	1998	2001	2001	2001	2001	2001
No role	4.2	3.4	2.9	5.4	2.6	2.2
Implementation role	16.8	11.6	14.3	16.1	7.7	13.0
Input role	49.6	43.8	48.6	46.4	43.6	39.1
Full partner	29.4	41.1	34.3	32.1	46.2	45.7

partnering when an organization is particularly focused on building its knowledge and intellectual capital.

The involvement of the HR function in business strategy can take a variety of forms. Table 1.5 shows that in 2001 virtually all HR functions report that they are involved in business strategy. When compared to 1998, an increase exists in the percentage of people who report that HR is involved as a full partner, but the difference is not statistically significant. Thus, the data suggest but do not establish that the HR function is becoming more of a strategic partner.

Involvement in strategy is highest in corporations that are in several sectors. One possible explanation is that, in several-sector business organizations, HR is in a position to add value by influencing strategy at both the corporate and sector levels. Large companies are more likely to have an HR function that is a business partner. This result is not surprising given that the HR issues in large companies are often more complex, and the HR function is more likely to be staffed with individuals who have a great deal of experience.

Table 1.6 shows the relationship between the strategic focus of organizations and the role HR plays in strategy. The results show a very consistent pattern. Regardless of whether growth, focus on the core business, quality and speed, or knowledge and information is the area of focus, more focus on strategy seems to exist when HR is a full partner rather than a minor one. This is particularly true with both the focus on quality and speed and the focus on knowledge and information. Thus, HR is particularly likely to be a strategic partner when the business strategy focus is one in which HR systems are critical.

Table 1.7 shows the relationship between change initiatives and the HR role in strategy. HR is more likely to be a full business partner in devel-

Table 1.6. Strategic Focuses and HR's Role in Strategy

	Growth	Core Business	Quality & Speed	Knowledge- & Information-Based Strategies
No role	2.5	2.0	2.9	2.9
Implementation role	2.3	2.8	3.3	3.6
Input role	2.9	2.4	3.7	3.8
Full partner	3.0	2.6	3.8	3.8

Means; response scale: 1 = little or no extent; 2 = some extent; 3 = moderate extent; 4 = great extent; 5 = very great extent.

Table 1.7. Change Initiatives and HR's Role in Strategy

	Restructuring	Organizational Performance	Competency & Knowledge Management
No role	3.7	2.1	1.9
Implementation role	3.4	2.9	2.6
Input role	3.2	2.9	2.8
Full partner	3.4	3.1	3.3

Means; response scale: 1 = little or no extent; 2 = some extent; 3 = moderate extent; 4 = great extent; 5 = very great extent.

oping strategy when organizations have a greater focus on initiatives that develop organizational performance and focus on competency and knowledge management. On the other hand, we found no relationship between the role of HR and the degree to which restructuring is a major change initiative.

Clearly, when HR has no role, restructuring is more likely to be an important initiative than are performance capability and knowledge management (3.7 versus 2.1 and 1.9). This raises an interesting question: Does HR influence the direction of the change initiatives, or do the change initiatives change HR's role? It may be that when HR has no role in planning strategy, organizations are more likely to focus on restructuring because HR does not acquaint them with the alternatives. Or it may be that when organizations focus on restructuring, they do not include HR in planning strategy because they feel that HR has little to contribute in this area. We tend to think the latter is the more common reason, but both probably do occur.

Overall, our data suggest that HR still has a considerable way to go in adding value as a business partner. It still spends a great deal of time on nonstrategic activities, just as it did in 1995. Even the numbers in Table 1.5, which show that over 40 percent of HR organizations play an important role in strategy, may be somewhat of an overestimation of the degree to which this occurs. The present study did not gather data from line managers to see how they would describe the role of HR in business strategy, but another study did ask both HR executives and line managers about how they see the role of HR (SHRM, 1998). It found a significant difference between HR executives' and line managers' estimates of the role they play in business. Not surprisingly, HR executives saw themselves playing more of a business-partner role than did line executives: 79 percent of the HR managers said they are business partners, whereas only 53 percent of the line managers shared this view.

SECTION 2

HR Organizational Approaches

The survey asked questions concerning the extent to which HR functions employ fifteen organizational and operational approaches. We chose these approaches for the study because they may facilitate HR being more of a business partner and in some cases a strategic partner. Statistical analysis divided the fifteen approaches into five groups. The groups and the mean responses to the items are shown in Table 2.1.

The practices used the least are self-funding of HR services and employee rotation into and out of HR. The lack of rotation is a major problem for the HR function. Without it, the HR staff are likely to remain a separate group that is not involved in or deeply knowledgeable about the business.

The practices used the most are those concerned with decentralization and service teams. Particularly popular is having decentralized generalists who support a business unit. This is a clear way to help HR become a business partner.

The moderate level of focus on resource efficiency is not surprising, given the financial challenges that most organizations faced in 2001. If anything, it is surprising that the focus on costs is not greater. Resource efficiency approaches include shared services, the transfer of tasks to line managers, self-service approaches, and self-funding requirements for HR services.

A comparison between the 1995 and 1998 results shows a significant increase in the use of three approaches: HR service teams, centers of excellence, and decentralized generalists. These same approaches show significant difference when we compare the 1995 and the 2001 results. Interestingly, the most frequently used approach, decentralized generalists, is also a practice that shows a significant increase. Clearly, companies want HR to be close to the business and act as a business partner, both at the corporate level and in individual business units.

The use of corporate centers of excellence is also increasing. This approach complements the use of decentralized generalists by giving them a source of expert help. Growth in the use of HR service teams is consistent with findings from other studies showing that teams grew in popularity during the 1990s (Lawler, Mohrman, and Benson, 2001).

Finally, the degree to which practices vary across business units has decreased. This may reflect efforts to simplify and achieve leverage in

Table 2.1. HR Organization

	Means		
	1995	1998	2001
Outsourcing	—	**2.2**	**2.2**
Transactional work is outsourced.	—	2.3	2.3
Areas of HR expertise are outsourced.	—	2.0	2.0
HR Service Teams	**2.9**	**3.3**	**3.3***
HR teams provide service and support the business.	2.9	3.4	3.5*
Corporate centers of excellence.	2.5	3.1	3.1*
HR systems and policies developed through joint line-HR task teams.	3.3	3.3	3.2
Decentralization	**3.2**	**3.1**	**3.2**
Decentralized HR generalists support business units.	3.6	3.9	4.0*
Very small corporate staff—most HR managers and professionals are out in businesses.	2.9	2.8	3.0
HR practices vary across business units.	2.9	2.6	2.6*
Resource Efficiency	—	**2.5**	**2.6**
Administrative processing is centralized.	3.5	3.4	3.4
Self-funding requirements exist for HR services.	1.7	1.9	1.9
Some activities that used to be done by HR are now done by line managers.	2.6	2.6	2.6
Some transactional activities that used to be done by HR are done by employees on a self-service basis.	—	2.3	2.5
Rotation	**2.1**	**2.2**	**2.1**
People rotate within HR.	2.6	2.8	2.8
People rotate into HR.	1.8	1.8	1.8
People rotate out of HR to other functions.	1.8	1.9	1.9

Response scale: 1 = little or no extent; 2 = some extent; 3 = moderate extent; 4 = great extent; 5 = very great extent.

* Significant difference ($p \leq .05$) between 1995 and 2001.

some HR activities and the tendency for companies to be in fewer diverse businesses. Corporations gain economies of scale when they use the same HR practices in all their units. As we will discuss later, this is particularly true in the case of transactions and the creation of IT-based self-service HR activities.

The relationship between companies' organizational structure and the organization of HR is shown in Table 2.2. Not surprisingly, single integrated businesses are less likely to deploy HR resources to the

Table 2.2. HR Organization and Organizational Structure

HR Organization	All Companies	Single Integrated Business	Multiple Related Business	Several-Sector Businesses	Large Companies
Outsourcing	2.2	2.1	2.3	2.0	2.3
HR service teams	3.3	3.2	3.4	3.2	3.5
Decentralization	3.2	2.9	3.3	3.4	3.5
Resource efficiency	2.6	2.4	2.8	2.6	2.9
Rotation	2.1	2.1	2.2	2.1	2.4

Means; response scale: 1 = little or no extent; 2 = some extent; 3 = moderate extent; 4 = great extent; 5 = very great extent.

business units than are the rest of the organizations in the sample. This finding fits directly with the view that multiple-business corporations need to have some variation in their HR policies by type of business and that there are fewer synergies in multiple-business corporations to support a centralized HR function. This interpretation is supported by the finding that HR practices are much less likely to vary across business units in a single integrated business than they are in the rest of the organizations in the sample.

Large companies do differ from small ones. Large companies are more likely to have small corporate staffs, use decentralized HR generalists, rotate people within the HR function, have self-funding, and have transactions done on a self-service basis. Not surprisingly, size has an impact on how HR is organized because size makes it possible for companies to capture economies of scale by having service centers, fund the development of advanced computer-based HR information systems (HRIS), and assign generalists to sectors of the company.

Table 2.3 shows how HR organizational approaches relate to strategic focus. One focus shows particularly strong results. When companies focus on growth, then decentralization, resource efficiency, HR service teams, and rotation all are more common. Rapidly growing organizations are under pressure to grow and develop their HR function. Decentralization, teams, and the development of individuals through rotation are all ways to add strategic and operational capability to the HR function. Resource-efficiency approaches may be required to prevent the HR function from being overwhelmed by the transactions that are required to staff and service a growing organization.

The use of HR service teams is significantly related to all of the strategic focuses; the relationship is particularly strong with knowledge- and

Table 2.3. Relationship of Strategic Focuses and Change Initiatives to Organization of HR

HR Organization	Strategic Focuses				Change Initiatives		
	Growth	Core Business	Quality & Speed	Knowledge- & Information-Based Strategies	Restructuring	Organizational Performance	Competency & Knowledge Management
Outsourcing	.15	.20*	.13	.13	.31***	.22**	.18*
HR service teams	.16*	.16*	.18*	.36***	.12	.33***	.41***
Decentralization	.39***	.17*	.13	-.01	.29***	.16	.18*
Resource efficiency	.20*	.14	.09	.12	.35***	.17*	.33***
Rotation	.28***	.13	.07	.08	.19*	.21*	.23**

Zero order correlation: * $p \leq 0.05$; ** $p \leq 0.01$; *** $p \leq 0.001$.

information-based strategies. The most likely reason for this is that strategy implementation often requires the development of cross-functional organizational and individual capabilities and the introduction of new organizational designs. Teams are one way to assemble the diversity of knowledge and skills required to address the complex HR issues that result.

Table 2.3 also shows the relationship between change initiatives and the organization of HR. A number of strong relationships are apparent. The use of outsourcing is related to all three change initiatives. This suggests that when an organization seriously addresses issues such as performance, restructuring, and knowledge management, it may free up HR resources by outsourcing, shedding transactional tasks, and securing external expertise to complement internal HR talent in order to implement these initiatives. Outsourcing also can be a way to reduce costs and improve service quality.

The use of HR service teams is significantly related to the organizational performance and competency and knowledge management initiatives. One likely reason for this is that HR service teams can bring together the multiple functions required to focus on performance improvement. At the same time, a team approach can improve competency and knowledge management in HR and in the rest of the organization.

Decentralization in HR is strongly related to restructuring. One possible reason for this is clear. When organizations restructure into multiple business units and complex business partnerships and networks, decentralization of HR is a way to establish a business partner relationship. It places the HR function close to its customers.

Resource-efficiency is significantly related to all three change initiatives. This suggests that whenever an organization considers change, a major issue is how to improve the efficiency of the HR organization. This is hardly surprising given the history of organizations being concerned about the cost of HR as a function and its administrative efficiency.

Rotation into and out of the HR function is significantly related to all three change initiatives. Focusing on major change initiatives may make it obvious to organizations that they can gain a considerable amount from having broader knowledge of HR in the organization and having individuals in HR who have a better understanding of the business. Rotation is one way to add to the knowledge and skills of HR professionals.

Overall, the results show relatively little change in the application of various organizational approaches from 1995 to 2001. We expected to see more adoption of practices such as joint line-HR development of HR systems, rotation, outsourcing, and centralized processing. These are all approaches that we believe can facilitate HR becoming more of a strategic partner, yet their use is not significantly increasing.

The results do strongly suggest that strategic change has significant and important effects on the HR organization. HR is likely to be significantly affected by change efforts that focus on issues like restructuring, organizational performance, and competency and knowledge management. In many respects, this is hardly surprising because HR is an important cost center in an organization and can add considerable value if it can become a strategic partner that supports these change initiatives. Given HR's history of not being a strategic partner, it is hardly surprising that efforts at restructuring often lead to changes in the HR function that appear to be targeted toward making HR more of a strategic partner.

SECTION 3

HR Activities

To get an in-depth sense of the changes that are occurring in the role of HR, we asked whether the focus on a number of HR activities has increased, stayed the same, or decreased over the past five to seven years. Data analyses showed five groups of HR activities and two activities that did not group with any other. Table 3.1 shows these activities and how companies responded in 1995, 1998, and 2001.

Our respondents reported the largest increases in focus (just as was true in 1995 and 1998) in the areas of organizational design, organizational development, recruitment, selection, compensation, and HRIS. They reported that their organizations' focus decreased in only two areas, union relations and record keeping (respondents rated both of these activities below "stayed the same" in 2001). Perhaps the most interesting finding is that, except for these two activities, companies report an increase in focus on the other seventeen activities. As HR functions take on new responsibilities, they do not seem to be decreasing their focus on most of their old ones.

A comparison of the 1995, 1998, and 2001 data shows some significant differences in the amount of increase reported. The largest increase is in recruitment and selection, a result that probably reflects the competition for talent that occurred during the 1990s and the growing focus in companies on attracting what some call "hot talent" and on being an employer of choice.

Three activities showed a significant decline: benefits, union relations, and affirmative action. This is not surprising. Union membership declined during this period, and benefits, particularly health care, were not as much an issue in 2001 as they were in the early 1990s, when benefit costs began to escalate. The slight decline for affirmative action probably reflects changes in the political and cultural environment.

We found no relationship between type of organizational structure and changes in the focus of HR activities. The forces leading to changes in the focus of HR functions do not seem to be related to the business configuration of the company. We also found no differences between large organizations and the rest of the sample.

Table 3.2 shows the relationships between activities and the four strategic focuses. A few significant relationships are apparent. Strategies that focus on quality and speed relate to an increased focus on design and organizational development, as well as to employee development. This

Table 3.1. Change in Focus on HR Activities During Past Five to Seven Years

	Means		
	1995	1998	2001
Design and Organizational Development	—	3.8	3.9
HR planning	4.1	3.9	4.0
Organizational development	4.0	3.8	3.9
Organizational design	—	3.6	3.7
Strategic planning	—	3.8	3.8
Compensation and Benefits	3.9	3.7	3.8
Compensation	3.9	3.8	3.9
Benefits	3.9	3.6	3.6*
Legal and Regulatory	—	3.1	3.1
Employee record keeping	2.8	2.8	2.7
Legal affairs	3.4	3.3	3.3
Affirmative action	3.3	3.1	3.1*
Employee assistance	—	3.1	3.2
Employee Development	—	—	3.6
Employee training/education	3.8	3.5	3.7
Management development	3.9	3.8	3.8
Performance appraisal	3.8	3.5	3.7
Career planning	3.3	3.4	3.3
Competency/talent assessment	—	—	3.7
Recruitment and Selection	3.4	3.9	3.8*
Recruitment	3.3	3.9	3.8*
Selection	3.5	3.8	3.7
HRIS	4.1	4.1	4.0
Union Relations	3.1	2.9	2.7*

Response scale: 1 = decreased; 3 = stayed the same; 5 = increased.

* Significant difference ($p \leq .05$) between 1995 and 2001.

Table 3.2. Relationship of Strategic Focuses and Change Initiatives to HR Activities

HR Activities	Strategic Focuses				Change Initiatives		
	Growth	Core Business	Quality & Speed	Knowledge- & Information- Based Strategies	Restructuring	Organizational Performance	Competency & Knowledge Management
Design and organizational development	.14	.06	.30***	.14	.02	.24**	.42***
Compensation and benefits	-.02	.07	.12	.15	.05	.12	.07
Legal and regulatory	-.09	-.02	.13	.05	-.11	.07	.08
Employee development	.02	.03	.32***	.29***	-.03	.29***	.40***
Recruitment and selection	.13	-.04	.14	.16	-.14	.10	.25**
HRIS	.09	.07	-.10	.08	-.08	.09	-.13
Union relations	-.01	-.18*	-.16	-.14	.04	.05	.03

Zero order correlation: * $p \leq 0.05$; ** $p \leq 0.01$; *** $p \leq 0.001$.

is not surprising because quality and speed are affected by cross-functional processes that can be addressed through new designs, skill development, and increased organizational alignment. In a similar vein, a knowledge and information strategy is associated with employee development. Both of these results suggest that business strategy does drive the activities of the HR function.

Two change initiatives are significantly correlated with changes in HR activities. Organizational performance initiatives are significantly related to design and organizational development and to employee development. These HR activities focus on key aspects of a firm's performance capabilities. Competency and knowledge management initiatives relate to three HR activities: design and organizational development, employee development, and recruitment and selection. These relationships reflect the importance of attracting and developing knowledge workers and of designing organizations for optimal application and leverage of knowledge. Together, these findings indicate ways in which HR is called upon to add value in the knowledge economy.

Surprisingly, neither growth nor the restructuring initiative is related to an increase in any of the HR activities. Because they clearly pose challenges in areas such as staffing, competency development, and organizational design, a relationship was expected. The lack of a relationship may be an indication that HR needs to make a better case for how its activities can support business strategy and organizational change.

Overall, the results do show changes in the focus of HR and a relationship between those changes and the strategic direction of the business. Particularly interesting is the increased focus on design and organizational development when certain change strategies and strategic focuses are present. This is an area that has not always been a focus of HR. It is, however, closely tied to organizational performance and business strategy. Providing expertise in this area may be a way for HR to become more of a business partner. Also of interest is the area of employee development, which is rated as an area of increased activity and is associated with two strategies and two change initiatives. It is clearly an increasingly important focus for HR functions. The increasing prevalence of strategies and initiatives that build on knowledge and employee competencies has opened the door for HR to become more of a strategic partner.

SECTION 4

Talent Strategies

Recruiting, developing, and retaining employees has always been a key HR focus. The importance of talent management has increased in the knowledge economy. Knowledge-based resources have replaced financial capital, natural resources, and unskilled labor as the most important source of competitive advantage. In the knowledge economy, human capital is critical to competitive advantage both because it is difficult for other firms to imitate and it is the critical determinant of performance (Jackson, Hitt, and DeNisi, 2003). Studies show that processes related to the management of human capital relate to firm financial performance (Hitt, Bierman, Shimizu, and Kochhar, 2001).

Much has been written about the "war for talent" (Michaels, Handfield-Jones, and Axelrod, 2001). Demographic trends such as the retirement of the baby-boomer generation and its replacement by a much smaller cohort suggest that labor markets for skilled knowledge workers will remain tight for several decades (Russell, 1993). To a great extent, firms "rent" the knowledge of their employees; they do not own it. An employee's knowledge walks out the door every evening and may not return. The value of knowledge workers to companies lies not only in their general knowledge—knowledge that they can apply in many settings—but also in the firm specific and tacit knowledge that they have developed through experience. Knowledge is embedded in the processes of the firm, and employee mastery of these processes is critical to effective performance. Furthermore, developing new performance capabilities requires introducing and improving work processes and developing new employee competencies.

Given that human capital is critical, developing an effective talent strategy may be the most important contribution that the HR function can make to the formation and implementation of business strategy. Indeed, in Section 3, we saw that firms continue to report an increase in attention to their recruitment and development responsibilities. These are key aspects of any talent strategy.

We added a new section to the survey in 2001, asking the extent to which various talent strategy practices are present. The seven practices divided into three groups. As Table 4.1 shows, they are development opportunities, management processes, and outplacement of lowest performers.

In the development arena, we see that 97 percent of firms use tuition reimbursement at least to some extent, with 53 percent reporting that they rely on this to a great or very great extent. Although 73 percent of

Table 4.1. Talent Strategy

	Percent Responding					Means
	Little or No Extent	Some Extent	Moderate Extent	Great Extent	Very Great Extent	
Development Opportunities						**2.6**
A significant investment in e-learning	27	32	21	15	5	2.4
Tuition reimbursement	3	17	27	33	20	3.5
A corporate university	59	13	14	5	9	1.9
Management Processes						**3.0**
Involvement by senior management	3	22	32	29	14	3.3
Regular talent reviews	10	19	28	27	16	3.2
Competency systems that are linked to HR practices	18	34	25	16	8	2.6
Outplacement of Lowest Performers	**16**	**28**	**23**	**23**	**10**	**2.8**

firms are using e-learning to some extent, only 20 percent of firms report that they are doing this to a great extent. Thus, e-learning appears to have gained a role in most companies, although perhaps not a major role. Additionally, 41 percent of firms are using a corporate university approach. Corporations using this approach usually offer a wide variety of courses internally. Judging from these results, many companies appear to be relying on employees to take responsibility for their own education, either by taking the initiative to take courses and degree programs or by taking advantage of electronic development activities.

Forty-three percent of the respondents say that senior management is to a great or very great extent involved in the management of talent and that regular talent reviews are to a great or very great extent part of their talent management processes. Fewer firms (24 percent) report that competency systems that are linked to their HR practices are a key part of their talent management strategy. These data suggest that although line management's role in the talent strategy is often in place, HR may be failing to provide an integrated competency system that enables a systematic approach to talent decisions.

Lately, it has become fashionable to suggest that firms should regularly weed out their lowest performers. Proponents argue that this makes room for good performers to advance, allows the company to bring in new blood, and results in continually raising performance standards. Our results suggest that most firms use this approach: 33 percent of firms report that outplacement or counseling out the lowest performers is to a great extent a part of their talent strategy, and 84 percent report that they do this at least to some extent.

We found no significant differences in the extent to which firms with different structures employ these talent strategies. Large companies do differ in two respects: they are more likely to have regular talent reviews, and they provide more development opportunities. Overall, the results indicate that large firms invest more in building their human capital.

Table 4.2 shows that the talent strategies are related to different business strategies and initiatives. The strongest relationships tend to be with knowledge- and information-based business strategies and with change initiatives focused on developing employee competencies and managing knowledge. Because tacit knowledge and deep expertise tend to be embodied to a large extent in people, strategies and initiatives that base competitiveness on leading in the knowledge arena inherently call for the development and deployment of talent. Similarly, strategies and initiatives that emphasize performance capabilities such as speed and quality depend heavily on the behavioral competencies of the workforce, that is, on having the talent to carry out new, more effective processes. Thus, it is not surprising that strategies and initiatives that require performance capabilities and behavioral competencies are related to the use of talent management practices.

Finally, the strategies and initiatives that emphasize knowledge are significantly related to the outplacement of the lowest performers. This fits with a focus on staffing the workforce with the most talented group of performers possible.

Strategies and initiatives that focus on growth, restructuring, and core businesses are generally not related to the use of various talent management strategies. There are exceptions, however. Growth and restructuring are both related to management processes, no doubt reflecting firms' need to fill new management positions and reconfigure talent when companies put new organizational configurations in place. Restructuring also is related to the outplacement of low performers, probably because they are the least likely to be offered opportunities in the new organization. Finally, a significant relationship exists between development strategies and a focus on the core business, probably because sticking to a core business reduces the variety of development that is

Creating a Strategic Human Resources Organization

Table 4.2. Relationship of Strategic Focuses and Change Initiatives to Talent Strategy

	Strategic Focuses				Change Initiatives		
	Growth	Core Business	Quality & Speed	Knowledge- & Information-Based Strategies	Restructuring	Organizational Performance	Competency & Knowledge Management
Development opportunities	.05	.17*	.21*	.26**	.12	.31***	.41***
Management processes	.17*	.08	.23**	.32***	.21*	.33***	.55***
Outplacement of lowest performers	.11	.11	.24**	.17*	.18*	.15	.17*

Zero order correlation: * $p \leq 0.05$; ** $p \leq 0.01$; *** $p \leq 0.001$.

required. In addition, it increases both the leverage of programs that are developed and the clarity about what development experiences are useful.

Others have argued that the knowledge economy contains large differences not only in the performance of different employees but also in their performance potential and their potential to add value. Much knowledge work is not routine in nature, requires the ability to solve complex problems and deal with ambiguity and uncertainty, and relies on the employee's initiative to deal with unstructured situations (Mohrman, Tenkasi, and Mohrman, 2000). These performance capabilities are not equally present, even among people with the same formal education and experience. In addition, although many skills are required for a knowledge firm to operate effectively, only some skills and knowledge are core, in the sense that they provide strategic and competitive advantage (Lepak and Snell, 2003).

Because of their importance, one can make the case for companies focusing a great deal of attention on identifying, nurturing, growing, and trying to retain employees with the most potential to add value to company performance. Fifty-seven percent of the companies in our sample report that they have special programs for high-potential employees.

We asked companies with high-potential programs to report on the extent to which these programs included seven approaches. The approaches divided into a development group and a rewards group (see Table 4.3). Most companies that have a program for high-potential employees include special development and assessment activities (88 percent) and special career development activities (82 percent), at least to a moderate extent. About two-thirds of the companies report moder-

Table 4.3. Use of Special Programs for High-Potential Employees

	Percent Responding					Means
	Little or No Extent	Some Extent	Moderate Extent	Great Extent	Very Great Extent	
Development						**3.0**
Job rotation programs	16	22	27	28	8	2.9
Special development and assessment activities	1	11	44	29	14	3.4
Special career development activities	5	13	38	37	8	3.3
Mentoring program	13	20	32	29	6	3.0
Providing a coach	18	30	34	9	9	2.6
Compensation						**1.8**
Special incentive programs	46	14	18	16	6	2.2
Individualized employment contracts	74	16	3	6	1	1.5

ate or greater use of mentoring and job rotation programs for high-potential employees, whereas about half report this same level of investment in providing coaches to these employees.

In comparison to development programs, companies are less likely to use special approaches to compensation and rewards as part of a program for high-potential employees. Still, we can expect that these employees might advance more quickly and thus receive favored salary treatment within the company's systems. Only 40 percent of companies with high-potential programs make moderate or more use of special incentives for this population, and only 10 percent make similar use of individualized employment contracts.

We found no significant differences in the use of various high-potential approaches by firms with different structures. Size does seem to make a difference in one area: large firms are more likely to have development activities. Two factors probably account for this: large firms have a greater need for talent development and more resources to devote to it.

Having a high-potential program is related to one strategy and one initiative (see Table 4.4). In particular, firms that have a high-potential program are more likely to have a growth strategy and to be restructur-

Table 4.4. Treatment of High-Potential Employees, Strategic Focuses, and Change Initiatives		
	Program of Special Treatment of High-Potential Employees	
	Yes	No
Strategic Focuses		
Growth	3.1	2.6*
Core business	2.6	2.3
Quality and speed	3.6	3.8
Knowledge- and information-based strategy	3.7	3.7
Change Initiatives		
Restructuring	3.5	3.1*
Organizational performance	3.0	2.9
Competency and knowledge management	3.0	2.9

Means; response scale: 1 = little or no extent; 2 = some extent; 3 = moderate extent; 4 = great extent; 5 = very great extent.

* Significant difference ($p \leq .05$) between the two categories.

ing than those that do not. Growth and restructuring may lead firms to spend more time identifying their high-potential talent and to invest in its development. Most likely, this is because these firms have the need to quickly develop talent to move into an increasing number of leadership positions.

If we look more closely within the population of firms that have a high-potential program (see Table 4.5), we see a more nuanced view of how the elements of such a program relate to strategy and change initiatives. Investment in special development and career support for high-potential employees does not relate to particular kinds of strategy. However, it does relate to the extent to which organizational performance and competency and knowledge management initiatives are in place. Thus, not only are firms with these initiatives more likely to make a large investment in development in general as part of their talent strategy, they are also likely to focus a great deal of their development investment on high-potential employees.

Using special compensation approaches as part of a company's high-potential program relates only to a strategy of focusing on the core

Table 4.5. Relationship of Strategic Focuses and Change Initiatives to High-Potential Practices

	Strategic Focuses				Change Initiatives		
	Growth	Core Business	Quality & Speed	Knowledge- & Information-Based Strategies	Restructuring	Organizational Performance	Competency & Knowledge Management
Development	.03	-.01	.10	.19	.09	.36***	.42***
Compensation	.16	.33**	.06	.06	.01	.09	.09

Zero order correlation: * $p \leq 0.05$; ** $p \leq 0.01$; *** $p \leq 0.001$.

Table 4.6. Relationship of Treatment of High-Potential Employees to Talent Strategy

	Talent Strategy		
	Development Opportunities	Management Processes	Ouplacement of Lowest Performers
Development	.30**	.49***	.09
Compensation	.15	.13	-.01

* Zero order correlation: * $p \leq 0.05$; ** $p \leq 0.01$; *** $p \leq 0.001$.

business. This strategy relies heavily on leading the market in a certain set of core competencies and a defined knowledge base. These firms can likely easily identify which talent is critical to such leadership and are willing to pay a great deal to retain that talent and keep it from going to competitors.

Table 4.6 shows the relationship between a talent strategy and the use of special development and compensation approaches for high-potential employees. Companies that have high-potential development programs are higher in the use of management processes associated with talent management. This is not surprising. Linking competency programs to the identification of high-potential employees and to targeting their development experiences and career moves ought to be a key part of any high-potential program. Also not surprising is the relationship between having development programs for individuals with high potential and having them for all employees.

Apparently, companies are either committed to talent development or they are not. Interestingly, the special compensation practice of some high-potential programs does not relate to the overall talent management practices. Finally, outplacement of the lowest performers is not more likely to be present in companies with high-potential programs.

In summary, we find strong evidence that firms are likely to invest in talent strategies when (1) their strategies are based on knowledge and information and on performance capabilities such as speed and quality, and (2) they have initiatives to support these focuses. Companies that have a growth strategy and are restructuring are the most likely to have a special program for high-potential employees. High-potential programs are more likely to have a strong development focus if the company also has knowledge and performance capability initiatives in place.

SECTION 5

Shared Services

Creating shared services units is one way to provide transactional HR services and specialized expertise to an organization's business units. Services may be shared in order to achieve efficiency, create a critical mass of expertise, and leverage knowledge resources. To determine what activities are being put in shared services units and how effective they are, our 1998 and 2001 surveys asked respondents questions about the use and effectiveness of a variety of shared services units. We asked survey takers from companies with a single business not to respond to this item because we are primarily interested in how frequently and effectively these units serve companies with more than one business unit. Table 5.1 shows the responses of companies with multiple units. Two groups of items emerged from our data analysis. One item, union relations, did not relate to these two groups.

Shared services units in companies offer a variety of transactional and expert services. Both the 1998 and 2001 results show that administrative services are more likely to be done by shared services units than are services concerned with development and management. Legal support, benefits administration, and HRIS are particularly likely to be performed through shared services units. This is not surprising because companies can capture significant economies of scale in the case of HRIS and benefits. In addition, companies may find advantages in knowledge management by concentrating technical expertise in one location.

The services that shared services units are particularly unlikely to provide are career planning, organizational development and design, and union relations. For the purposes of knowledge management, it may make sense for firms to use shared services in these areas. On the other hand, these are areas that often require deeper familiarity with particular business units and a close relationship with clients. Thus, perhaps the best approach for them is to create small centralized services units and to place individual specialists in business units. Alternatively, some of these functions may be provided by the HR generalists who are in the businesses.

The finding that employee training and management development are only moderately likely to be performed by shared services units is somewhat surprising. These are areas where the potential certainly exists for centralizing expertise, achieving economies of scale through sharing development activities, and creating centers of excellence. Perhaps what

Creating a Strategic Human Resources Organization

Table 5.1. Use of Shared Services by Companies with Multiple Business Units

	Percent Responding			Means	
	Not at All	Some Shared Service	Entirely Through Shared Service	1998[1]	2001[2]
Administrative Services				**2.3**	**2.2**
Employee record keeping	23	45	33	2.2	2.1
Legal support	18	35	47	2.4	2.3
Compensation	17	46	37	2.3	2.2
Benefits	9	35	56	2.6	2.5
HRIS	17	29	54	2.5	2.4
Affirmative action	28	38	34	2.2	2.1
Development Services				**1.8**	**1.8**
Recruitment and selection	37	50	13	1.9	1.8
Career planning	63	23	14	1.4	1.5
Organizational development and design	47	33	20	1.8	1.7
Employee training	21	59	19	1.9	2.0
Management development	32	45	23	1.9	1.9
Union Services (Relations)	**52**	**30**	**18**	**1.9**	**1.7**

[1] N = 94. [2] N = 111.

companies are doing is combining some local services that are close to the customer with centralized, corporate, shared services that deal with overall corporate issues and provide resources to the business unit. This approach may be particularly appropriate in multiple-business corporations that are in diverse businesses because each of the businesses has somewhat specialized needs.

A comparison between the use of shared services in 1998 and 2001 shows no significant differences. As Table 5.1 indicates, the largest change is a small decrease in the use of union shared services units. Apparently, shared services have not increased in popularity since 1998.

The use of shared services was the same for related business organizations and business sector organizations. This is a bit surprising because one would expect companies with different sectors to have a larger diversity of requirements than those with multiple related businesses—a factor that might be expected to work against both the use and effec-

Table 5.2. Effectiveness of Shared Services in Companies with Multiple Business Units					
	Percent Responding			Means	
	Not Effective	Somewhat Effective	Very Effective	1998[1]	2001[2]
Administrative Services				**2.5**	**2.5**
Employee record keeping	9	28	63	2.5	2.5
Legal support	5	22	73	2.7	2.7
Compensation	5	29	66	2.6	2.6
Benefits	3	36	61	2.7	2.6
HRIS	11	50	39	2.2	2.3
Affirmative action	12	29	59	2.5	2.5
Development Services				**2.2**	**2.3**
Recruitment and selection	8	47	45	2.4	2.4
Career planning	19	67	13	1.8	1.9
Organizational development and design	14	55	31	2.2	2.2
Employee training	6	56	38	2.2	2.3
Management development	9	53	38	2.3	2.3
Union Services (Relations)	**13**	**20**	**67**	**2.7**	**2.5**

[1] N = 94. [2] N = 111.

tiveness of sharing services. We also found no relationship between organization size and the use of shared services. This is a bit surprising because larger organizations would seem to be better positioned to create and gain from such sharing.

Table 5.2 shows the shared services' level of effectiveness. Respondents saw all the services as being at least somewhat effective. One area, career planning, stands out with a particularly low rating. This finding, combined with the low use of shared career-planning services, suggests that this function may need to be tailored to the needs of different business units or populations. Or it may reflect organizations' overall lack of attention to developing high-quality career development systems. It is possible that career development services would currently receive low effectiveness ratings whether delivered through shared services or not.

On the positive side, legal support, union relations, affirmative action, and benefits all get high effectiveness ratings. Not too far behind are compensation and employee record keeping. Interestingly enough, some highly rated shared services provide expertise and some provide transactions. Apparently, shared services units can effectively provide both transaction services and expert advice and knowledge, although the transaction services rate most highly overall.

A comparison between the 1998 and 2001 effectiveness data shows no significant change in the effectiveness of the shared services units. The largest change is a statistically insignificant decrease in the union area, the one area where shared services use is declining.

A comparison of the effectiveness of shared services units among organizations with different structures found no significant differences. We did find a slight tendency for larger organizations to report that their shared services units are more effective. This makes sense because larger organizations may be able to put more resources into developing shared services units. Likewise, they may be able to extract significant economies of scale that heavily influence HR executives' perceptions of their effectiveness.

Table 5.3 shows that the use and effectiveness of shared services have little relationship to strategic focuses and no relationship to change initiatives. The only significant relationship is that using shared services for union relations is less common when the company has growth strategies and strategies that focus on the core business. Companies probably are attempting to grow without extending unionization. This would lead to trying to contain unions in local pockets and to treating union relations as a local issue.

Overall, shared services are most likely to be used to deliver administrative services such as HRIS and benefits. They are also frequently used to provide legal support. Development services are much less likely to be provided by shared services units.

We found no evidence that the use of any shared services units increased from 1998 to 2001, despite our earlier finding that companies reported making greater use of centers of excellence. The most likely explanation for this seeming inconsistency is that the use of centers of excellence is increasing, possibly because they support knowledge management, whereas the use of other kinds of shared services units are not. This interpretation is supported by the finding in Section 2 that organizations are not making greater use of centralized administrative processing units.

The results suggest that shared services units are particularly likely to be effective when they are used for transactional work. Finally, the results show no increase in the effectiveness of shared services units.

Table 5.3. Relationship of Strategic Focuses and Change Initiatives to Use and Effectiveness of Shared Services

	Strategic Focuses				Change Initiatives		
	Growth	Core Business	Quality & Speed	Knowledge- & Information-Based Strategies	Restructuring	Organizational Performance	Competency & Knowledge Management
Shared Services Use							
Administrative services	-.14	.02	-.06	.02	.01	.09	-.07
Development services	-.06	-.04	.02	.06	-.06	.12	.14
Union services (relations)	-.22*	-.30**	.03	.05	-.05	.11	-.14
Effectiveness of Shared Services							
Administrative services	.01	.16	.19	.18	.20	.15	.12
Development services	.22	.07	-.07	.10	.32	.07	.13
Union services (relations)	.21	.12	.13	.20	.08	.09	.16

Zero order correlation: * $p \leq 0.05$; ** $p \leq 0.01$; *** $p \leq 0.001$.

For some services where building expertise in each business unit does not make sense, an alternative to creating an internal shared services unit is outsourcing. Outsourcing may in effect create the equivalent of shared services in vendor firms. Our study also investigated the use of outsourcing, and we will describe the results in Section 6.

SECTION 6

Outsourcing

Outsourcing is one way that a company can improve the effectiveness of an HR function. In addition to acquiring the expertise of skilled HR professionals, the company that uses outsourcing can reduce both the transactional work of HR organizations and costs. In the best-case scenario, outsourcing companies can provide better and cheaper services because they are focused on a particular process or area of expertise that is their core competency, and they can capture economies of scale by providing this service to multiple organizations. They also can improve the processes of organizations because of the knowledge they have. At the very least, outsourcing can reduce the number of employees who are on the HR department payroll and can create a flexible cost structure when the company needs services occasionally or for short periods.

Table 6.1 shows the degree to which companies are currently outsourcing eighteen HR activities. The activities are divided into the five groups that our statistical analysis produced; seven items did not group. In 1995, 1998, and 2001, the use of outsourcing varied widely among these activities, but in no case was any of them even close to being completely outsourced.

Over 90 percent of the companies did not outsource HR planning, strategic planning, organizational design, and performance appraisal at all. These are all areas where HR can add considerable strategic value and act as a strategic partner. However, they are not all areas where HR is very active (for example, strategic planning and organizational design).

Most likely to be outsourced was employee assistance, an area that over 50 percent of the companies completely outsourced. This is hardly surprising given its personal and confidential nature. Benefits was next, with over 80 percent of the companies partially or completely outsourcing the area. The frequency of outsourcing of benefits probably reflects the combination of transitional and specialized knowledge work that it involves. In over 50 percent of the companies, training, recruitment, and legal affairs were partially or completely outsourced.

The use of outsourcing includes areas where extensive expertise is involved, such as legal affairs, and areas where primarily transactional work occurs, such as benefits administration. This provides confirmation that organizations are outsourcing to gain both transactional efficiency and expertise.

A comparison among the 1995, 1998, and 2001 results shows a general,

Table 6.1. Outsourcing Use						
	Percent Responding			Means		
	Not at All	Partially	Completely	1995	1998	2001
Planning				—	1.1	1.1
HR planning	96	4	0	1.0	1.1	1.0
Strategic planning	93	7	0	—	1.1	1.1
Organizational Design/Development					1.2	1.2
Organizational development	77	21	2	1.3	1.3	1.2
Organizational design	91	8	1	—	1.2	1.1
Training				1.6	1.7	1.7*
Employee training/education	26	73	2	1.6	1.9	1.8
Management development	41	59	1	1.5	1.6	1.6
HRIS and Record Keeping				1.2	1.5	1.4*
HRIS	54	43	3	1.3	1.6	1.5*
Employee record keeping	73	26	1	1.2	1.4	1.3
Staffing and Career Development				1.2	1.2	1.2
Performance appraisal	93	6	1	1.0	1.1	1.1*
Recruitment	49	50	2	1.4	1.6	1.5*
Selection	83	17	1	1.2	1.2	1.2
Career planning	86	14	1	1.1	1.2	1.2
Benefits	19	72	9	1.7	1.9	1.9*
Compensation	55	44	1	1.2	1.5	1.5*
Legal Affairs	44	51	5	1.4	1.6	1.6*
Affirmative Action	68	30	2	1.1	1.2	1.3*
Employee Assistance	20	26	54	—	2.2	2.3
Competency/Talent Assessment	68	31	1	—	—	1.3
Union Relations	86	14	0	1.1	1.1	1.1

* Significant difference ($p \leq .05$) between 1995 and 2001.

although small, increase in the use of outsourcing. Specifically, the following areas show statistically significant increases in the use of outsourcing from 1995 to 2001: compensation, benefits, employee training, HRIS, recruitment, performance appraisal, affirmative action, and legal affairs. No activity was less likely to be outsourced in 2001 than it was in 1995. Thus, it is safe to conclude that a trend toward outsourcing may just be beginning to unfold. Clearly, the opportunity

Creating a Strategic Human Resources Organization

for more outsourcing to take place is great, because only a very few companies completely outsource any of their HR activities.

The results show no significant differences in the outsourcing behavior of the various types of organizations. This is not surprising because outsourcing is likely to be equally effective in the different organizational structures we studied.

Table 6.2 presents the responses to a question about the type of problems that resulted from outsourcing. The eleven items divided into two groups. The data suggest that companies have experienced a number of problems in their outsourcing activities, although the majority of companies do not experience them to a great extent or very great extent. The most common problems involve contractor and administrative issues. Over 50 percent of the firms say that to a moderate or great extent administering the outsourcing activity is more expensive than executives expected; the services have not been as good as promised; the costs are higher than promised; and contractors do not have enough knowledge of the company. Over 40 percent say that the switch to alternative outsourcers is difficult, and they lack skills in managing contractors. The picture that emerges is one of companies experiencing significant problems with outsourcing but finding it difficult to switch to alternative vendors. Particularly disturbing are the reports of high costs and poor quality.

It is not surprising that the frequency of contractor problems is high, given the general lack of experience that HR executives have in contracting for services. As we noted, these organizations recognize that they sometimes lack the skills to deal with contractors.

The problem that occurs least frequently is the loss of competitive advantage from the way companies manage people. This is a bit surprising because allowing outsourcers to deliver HR services can change the relationship between employees and organizations. Outsourcing HR can depersonalize and homogenize the relationship so that organizations lose part of their brand as an employer.

We can think of three possible explanations for why organizations may not feel they are losing competitive advantage. First, the outsourcing may involve transactional work that is not a key strategic interface with the employees. Second, the organizations may have carefully structured their outsourcing arrangements so that their HR programs have unique features that foster the kind of relationship they want with their employees. Third, many organizations may never have managed their people in a way that gave them a competitive advantage, so they had little to lose by outsourcing.

Table 6.2. Problems in Managing Outsourcing

	Percent Responding					Means	
	Little or No Extent	Some Extent	Moderate Extent	Great Extent	Very Great Extent	1998	2001
Contractor and Administrative Issues						**2.4**	**2.5**
Resources required to manage the contract and relationship have been more than anticipated.	19	28	30	21	1	2.5	2.6
Services haven't been as good as promised.	9	30	39	20	1	2.7	2.7
Contractors don't know enough about the company.	17	30	32	18	3	2.4	2.6
Cost has been higher than promised.	14	26	39	18	3	2.5	2.7
Lack of skills for managing contractors.	29	31	26	10	4	2.4	2.3
Switch to new outsourcers is very difficult.	29	30	24	14	3	2.3	2.3
Effectiveness of Outsourcing						**2.0**	**2.0**
Loss of competitive advantage from the way we manage people	53	24	13	8	2	1.6	1.8
Negative reaction from business units served	38	35	19	7	1	2.0	2.0
Negative reaction from company employees	30	40	20	7	2	2.1	2.1
Negative reaction from HR employees	36	33	20	8	2	2.1	2.1
Can't have HR systems we need	40	29	10	14	7	2.1	2.2

No significant difference ($p \leq .05$) between time periods.

Comparison of the 1998 and 2001 responses shows a slight, not statistically significant, increase in problems in several areas. In 2001, companies are more likely to report that contractors do not know enough about the company and that costs have been higher than promised. Neither of these results is particularly surprising because an organization can assess how much a contractor knows and is willing to learn about its functioning only after the contractor gets in place. Further, although costs may not rise during the period of the initial contract, contractors may try to negotiate a higher price upon renewal, particularly if they have used a

Creating a Strategic Human Resources Organization

Table 6.3. Relationship of Strategic Focuses and Change Initiatives to Outsourcing

	Strategic Focuses				Change Initiatives		
	Growth	Core Business	Quality & Speed	Knowledge- & Information-Based Strategies	Restructuring	Organizational Performance	Competency & Knowledge Management
Overall outsourcing (all items)	.04	.12	.16	-.03	.30***	.23*	.11
Planning	-.12	-.02	-.06	.05	.01	.07	-.02
Oganizational design/development	-.00	.07	.17	.17	.15	.28**	.10
Training	.10	.10	.12	.01	.26**	.11	.13
HRIS and record keeping	.04	.19*	.09	-.05	.21*	.20*	.14
Staffing and career development	.05	.06	.02	.07	.15	.14	.03
Benefits	.04	.17*	.06	.05	.18*	.15	.07
Compensation	-.02	.06	.15	.05	.15	.17	.04
Legal affairs	-.04	-.01	.06	-.15	.23**	.08	.11
Affirmative action	-.01	.04	-.06	-.10	.12	-.03	-.03
Employee assistance	-.07	-.05	.11	-.07	.11	.03	.04
Competency/talent assessment	-.02	.11	.07	-.01	.06	.17	.06
Union relations	-.13	-.02	-.07	-.02	-.08	.06	.12

Zero order correlation: * $p \leq 0.05$; ** $p \leq 0.01$; *** $p \leq 0.001$.

low price to gain entry into the organization. Finally, the item concerned with loss of competitive advantage shows a slightly higher score in 2001 than in 1998. One possibility is that as organizations become more familiar with all of the implications of outsourcing, they then find that this is a more pressing concern for them.

These organizations raised enough concerns regarding outsourcing for us to issue some cautions. Before they outsource, organizations need to develop the capability to manage contractors and have adequate internal resources to manage them. Costs are also a critical issue; organizations need to pay particular attention to cost control in this area.

Table 6.3 shows that very few significant relationships exist between strategic focus and outsourcing. The lack of a relationship between growth strategies and outsourcing is surprising, especially given our findings in 1998 that growth-focused organizations were more likely to outsource than were other organizations. Growth puts stress on an organization's HR delivery capabilities, and outsourcing could provide a quick way to acquire additional support for an HR function that is under pressure to serve a larger organization. It is not clear why this relationship is not present in the 2001 data.

Two of the change initiatives are related to outsourcing behavior. Restructuring in particular is strongly related to overall outsourcing, as well as to the outsourcing of training, HRIS, benefits, and legal affairs. Understanding why restructuring might lead to greater outsourcing is not hard: serious restructuring efforts question the way a number of tasks are done in an organization and often involve looking for cheaper and better alternatives. Outsourcing is a viable alternative and in some cases can lead to lower costs, thus becoming an element of a restructuring program.

Organizational performance initiatives are also related to outsourcing overall, as well as to the outsourcing of HRIS and organizational design. Apparently, when organizations focus on performance, they seek outside help in organizational design and find that outsourcing is a way to improve performance.

Overall, outsourcing is clearly growing slowly and is likely to continue to grow. It fits with organizations being in a growth mode and with the desire of many HR organizations to get out of transaction and service activities so that they can become more of a strategic business partner. Outsourcing also allows organizations to gain access to knowledge and expertise that they do not have and are not in a good position to develop. A potential obstacle to the growth of outsourcing is the number of problems associated with it, including the apparent difficulty of getting sustained cost and quality advantages. So far, none of the obstacles seems to have been severe enough to prevent the growth in outsourcing, but the fact that they are increasing in frequency could signal future problems for outsourcing.

SECTION 7

Use of IT

IT is a potentially powerful way to accomplish HR record keeping, HR transactions, and many other tasks efficiently and accurately, thus enabling HR managers to spend more time on strategic business support. IT may be a way to deliver expert advice to managers and employees in areas such as selection, career development, and compensation. It may also facilitate change efforts by assessing the capabilities of the workforce and by providing information and training that supports change. Finally, it can support the development of business strategy by providing important information about the organization's capabilities and core competencies.

Table 7.1 shows the current state of IT-based HR processes in the companies we studied. Forty-four percent of companies use IT for most or all of their HR systems, and 92 percent have at least some IT-based processes. This is a relatively high level of IT use.

We were surprised to find no increase in IT use from 1995 to 2001. We cannot account for why this is, particularly in light of the large amount of activity that seems to be occurring in the eHR world. One possible explanation is that organizations are making investments in eHR, but their investments are focused on improving the functionality of the processes that already use IT (for example, benefits administration and employee record keeping) rather than on adding new processes.

The extent of IT use is not strongly related to type of business configuration, nor is it related to an organization's size. That said, we should note that single-business companies are the least likely to have most HR processes based in IT. This is a surprising finding, particularly because it was not the case in our 1995 and 1998 studies. It is also surprising that the largest organizations in our sample are not significantly greater IT users. They are likely to have more resources to put into the development of eHR systems and can achieve greater economies of scale. One explanation for this is that even the smaller organizations in our sample have thousands of employees and thus may have enough size to justify using IT in their HR function.

In 1998, we added a second question on the use of company computer-based information systems to our survey to get a more complete picture of the systems' capabilities. It asked about the degree to which employees and/or managers could perform certain HR tasks by way of a computer-based information system. Table 7.2 shows the results for 1998 and 2001 grouped on the basis of a statistical analysis. Perhaps the

Table 7.1. State of HR IT

	Percent Responding						
	1995	**1998**	**2001**	**Single Integrated Business**	**Multiple Related Business**	**Several-Sector Businesses**	**Large Companies**
Little or no IT/automation present in the HR function	6.3	8.4	8.3	10.8	3.7	15.8	4.3
Some HR processes are IT-based/automated	45.3	40.3	48.3	56.8	46.3	36.8	47.8
Most processes are IT-based/automated but not fully integrated	40.6	42.9	35.9	29.7	38.9	39.5	39.1
Completely integrated HR IT/automated system	7.8	8.4	7.6	2.7	11.1	7.9	8.7

most striking finding is the variation in the extent to which these HR activities that employees and managers can perform with computer-based systems. The most frequent are posting job openings, applying for jobs, arranging for travel reimbursements, and changing benefits. At the other extreme are eight activities that, in over 50 percent of the companies, employees cannot do on the computer systems at all. Many of these are in the management tool group.

What most clearly distinguishes the tasks that are frequently done from those that are not is the degree to which the activities are transactional. Transactional activities are particularly likely to be done on a computer system, whereas those involving expert advice and decision making (for example, all the management tool items) are either done not at all or only partially by way of computerized information systems. This difference is hardly surprising, because transactions are particularly suited to self-service. To offer advice takes much more sophisticated software support, although there are many ongoing efforts to create expert systems that can help with career development, management training, and new-hire orientation. In the future, individuals will increasingly serve themselves with computer-based information systems.

A comparison between the 1998 and 2001 results shows significant increases in the ability to do four activities. Particularly noticeable is the increased ability to use computer systems for job information. Organizations have increasingly adopted the Web as a way to handle the job application and job-posting processes. We also find evidence of increased use of the computer for performance management. This may well reflect the use of computers for 360-degree appraisals and for generally accumulating performance data throughout an organization.

Table 7.3 shows that in most areas the large organizations in our sample

Creating a Strategic Human Resources Organization

Table 7.2. Computer System Activities Done by Employees or Managers					
	Percent Responding			Means	
Use Computer Systems for	Not at All	Partially	Completely	1998	2001
Personnel Records					**2.1**
Change benefit coverage	24	33	43	2.2	2.2
Change address and/or other personal information	32	27	41	2.0	2.1
Job Information					**2.1**
Apply for a job (external applicants)	23	34	43	1.9	2.2*
Apply for a job (internal applicants)	22	33	45	1.5	2.2*
Post job openings	10	26	64	1.5	2.5*
Post personal résumé/bio	62	26	12	—	1.5
Financial Transactions					**1.9**
Travel and expense reimbursements	25	29	46	—	2.2
Purchase products and services from vendors	52	36	12	—	1.6
Employee Training					**1.7**
New-hire orientation	61	34	6	—	1.5
Technical skills training	37	54	9	—	1.7
Scheduling training and development	27	47	26	—	2.0
Management Tools					**1.5**
Career development planning	63	29	9	1.4	1.5
Obtain advice and information on handling personnel issues	56	39	6	1.5	1.5
Identifying management development resources	51	37	13	—	1.6
Management development training	55	41	5	—	1.5
Search for employees with specified skills/competencies	62	30	8	—	1.5
Salary Planning/Administration	**26**	**52**	**22**	**1.9**	**2.0**
Performance Management	**30**	**53**	**17**	**1.5**	**1.9***

* Significant difference ($p \leq .05$) between 1998 and 2001.

are somewhat more likely to use computer systems than are other organizations. The difference is statistically significant in the case of financial transactions and job information. A possible explanation for this is the magnitude and complexity of such tasks in large businesses and the significant aid that a computer-based system can provide because it facilitates data gathering, retrieval, and storage. It also provides some obvious economies of scale. Table 7.3 does not show any relationship between organization structure and computer system activities.

Table 7.4 shows the relationship between the strategic focuses and change initiatives in an organization and the kind of activities that are done on the computer. The table indicates relatively few significant relationships. Not surprisingly, growth is related to the use of comput-

Table 7.3. Computer System Activities and Organization Structure

	All Companies	Single Integrated Business	Multiple Related Business	Several-Sector Businesses	Large Companies
Use Computer Systems for					
Personnel records	2.1	2.1	2.1	2.1	2.3
Job information	2.1	2.1	2.2	2.1	2.3
Financial transactions	1.9	1.9	1.9	1.9	2.1
Employee training	1.7	1.7	1.7	1.8	1.8
Management tools	1.5	1.4	1.5	1.6	1.5
Salary planning/administration	2.0	1.6	1.9	2.2	2.1
Performance management	1.9	1.7	1.9	2.0	2.0

Means; response scale: 1 = not at all; 2 = partially; 3 = completely.

Table 7.4. Relationship of Strategic Focuses to Computer System Use

	Strategic Focuses				Change Initiatives		
	Growth	Core Business	Quality & Speed	Knowledge- & Information-Based Strategies	Restructuring	Organizational Performance	Competency & Knowledge Management
Use Computer Systems for							
Personnel records	.05	-.03	-.05	.07	.04	.01	.08
Job information	.14	.20*	-.03	.12	.02	-.08	.08
Financial transactions	.14	.01	-.03	.14	.10	.04	.04
Employee training	.10	.13	.02	.06	.11	.02	.06
Management tools	.19*	.14	-.03	.15	.15	.15	.27***
Salary planning/administration	.23**	.01	-.05	.05	.20*	.06	.04
Performance management	.11	.02	-.00	.25**	.06	.11	.14

Zero order correlations: * $p \leq 0.05$; ** $p \leq 0.01$; *** $p \leq 0.001$.

ers for salary administration. One of the advantages of a computer-based salary administration system is scalability, so it makes sense that a company would more likely use computers when growth is part of the organization's strategy.

The results show an interesting relationship between computer system use and change initiatives. Organizations with competency and knowledge management initiatives are particularly likely to make computerized management tools available. Tools for managers' self-development

Table 7.5. Computer System Effectiveness

Computer Systems Effective for	Percent Responding			Means	
	Not Effective	Somewhat Effective	Very Effective	1998	2001
Personnel Records					**2.6**
Change benefit coverage	7	31	62	2.5	2.6
Change address and/or other personal information	8	31	62	2.4	2.5
Job Information					**2.2**
Apply for a job (external applicants)	9	47	44	2.1	2.4*
Apply for a job (internal applicants)	9	40	51	1.8	2.4*
Post job openings	7	39	54	1.8	2.5*
Post personal résumé/bio	40	43	17	—	1.8
Financial Transactions					**2.1**
Travel and expense reimbursements	15	36	49	—	2.3
Purchase products and services from vendors	21	53	27	—	2.1
Employee Training					**2.1**
New-hire orientation	25	57	18	—	1.9
Technical skills training	12	61	27	—	2.2
Scheduling training and development	10	51	38	—	2.3
Management Tools					**1.8**
Career development planning	29	57	13	1.7	1.8
Obtain advice and information on handling personnel issues	24	59	17	1.8	1.9
Identifying management development resources	18	62	20	—	2.0
Management development training	27	63	10	—	1.8
Search for employees with specified skills/competencies	43	47	11	—	1.7
Salary Planning/Administration	**7**	**49**	**44**	**2.2**	**2.4***
Performance Management	**14**	**59**	**26**	**1.8**	**2.1***

* Significant difference ($p \leq .05$) between 1998 and 2001.

and tools that provide information useful in managing and developing employees may best be thought of as part of the infrastructure for knowledge management and competency development.

The results concerned with the effectiveness of computer systems (see Table 7.5) mirror those concerned with their availability. Computer systems are least effective when they provide management tools; they are most effective when they involve personnel records, salary administration, and job information. Again, this is hardly surprising. These activities have been on IT-based systems for a longer time and in most cases involve simpler transactions.

Table 7.6. Relationship of Strategic Focuses to Computer System Effectiveness

	Strategic Focuses				Change Initiatives		
	Growth	Core Business	Quality & Speed	Knowledge- & Information-Based Strategies	Restructuring	Organizational Performance	Competency & Knowledge Management
Computer Systems Effective for							
Personnel records	.10	-.01	-.01	.05	-.01	-.12	-.00
Job information	.09	.27*	.05	.20	.02	.04	.19
Financial transactions	.13	.09	-.08	.08	.13	-.12	.03
Employee training	.16	.24	.06	.12	.16	.04	.22
Management tools	.31	.17	-.01	.15	.16	.05	.36*
Salary planning/administration	.14	.01	-.07	.12	.05	.12	.24*
Performance management	.10	-.05	.10	.09	.08	.10	.05

Zero order correlations: * $p \leq 0.05$; ** $p \leq 0.01$; *** $p \leq 0.001$.

Comparing the 1998 with the 2001 effectiveness results shows five significant increases in effectiveness and no decreases. The increases in the job information area are especially noticeable. Apparently, computerized job-posting and job application processes have improved tremendously in most of these companies. Performance management and salary administration systems also show increased effectiveness. These results suggest that improvement occurs as organizations become more familiar with and have more experience with IT-based HR systems.

We found no significant relationships between the effectiveness of IT systems and organization structure. There is a significant but small tendency for large organizations to report higher effectiveness levels in three areas: salary administration, personnel records, and job information. Again, this may well reflect the resources that large organizations have and their ability to buy and develop better systems, as well as the considerable economies of scale and consequent cost savings that they may experience.

Table 7.6 relates the effectiveness of computer systems to a company's strategic focuses and change initiatives. There are relatively few significant results here. One interesting result concerns change initiatives: competency and knowledge management initiatives are significantly correlated with the effectiveness of management tools. This is a similar finding to the earlier finding about the relationship of computer use to change initiatives. Apparently, having a change initiative concerned with competency and knowledge management relates to providing

Table 7.7. Relationship of Change in HR Activity to Computer Use and Effectiveness

	HR Activity Change					
	Design & Organizational Development	Compensation & Benefits	Legal & Regulatory	Employee Development	Recruitment & Selection	HRIS
Use Computer Systems for						
Personnel records	-.03	-.02	-.14	-.03	-.02	.07
Job information	.03	.17*	-.03	.09	.06	.16
Financial transactions	.11	.06	-.12	.10	-.06	.18*
Employee training	-.03	.07	-.06	.04	.01	.14
Management tools	.12	.25**	-.03	.17*	.03	.18*
Salary planning/administration	-.09	.02	-.07	-.06	-.07	.17*
Performance management	.10	-.03	-.16	.27***	.06	.06

* Zero order correlations: $*\, p \leq 0.05$; $**\, p \leq 0.01$; $***\, p \leq 0.001$

online management tools and is associated with their being more effectively used.

IT is a key enabling component of most knowledge management initiatives. Thus, it is not surprising that a company with knowledge management and competency development as an explicit focus is more likely both to provide computerized management tools and use them effectively. Indeed, in order to be effective, a change initiative in this area may very well require the use of IT.

The increased use of IT for transactional and other HR services may free up the time of HR professionals and shift their focus away from transactions to more value-added business partner activities. Computerized systems also may complement the work of HR professionals and form an integral part of new or enhanced HR focuses and services. If either of these is true, we should see a relationship between the extent of use of IT approaches and the change in emphasis on various HR activities. Table 7.7 shows the relationship between the use of IT for various purposes and changes in the emphasis and activities of the HR function.

As we might expect, greater emphasis on HRIS is related to the use of IT for three self-service purposes. Two of the exceptions—personnel records and performance management—are the most interesting. Most companies have been working for years on computer applications for changing personal information and benefits coverage, so it may be that these applications do not represent an increased emphasis on HRIS.

Performance management applications are related to an increased emphasis on employee development but nothing else. One reason for this may be that computer systems for performance management are often tailor-made for use in a separate development process and may not be integral to the overall HRIS. Interestingly, computer performance management applications are slightly negatively related to increases in a company's focus on legal and regulatory issues. This may reflect the conservative influence of lawyers, who worry about issues such as increased traceability of potentially incriminating data or about legal defensibility of employee ratings that are impersonally created by a variety of people who do not have management responsibility for the person they are rating.

Posting of job information is related to increased emphasis on compensation and benefits. Computerizing the posting of jobs and résumés and the application process may get HR out of the loop for the transactional parts of hiring and selection. Thus, it may enable a greater focus on the attendant issues of compensation. Computerized applications also probably create a visibility to the hiring process that drives more attention to the highly charged issues of the underlying compensation philosophy, systems, and administration.

The computerized applications most related to change in HR focus are those pertaining to management tools. The use of these tools is related to increases in emphasis on compensation and benefits and employee development. Thus, it appears that the computer systems can operate as an integral part of the value that HR delivers in these areas.

Computerized applications are not significantly related to changes in emphasis in two HR activities: (1) recruitment and selection and (2) legal and regulatory. The latter is not surprising because most computerized applications (with the possible exception of those that provide legal information and advice to managers) do not directly deal with these domains. Recruitment and selection is a bit surprising, although companies are probably pursuing the computerization of job information for efficiency purposes regardless of whether they are increasing the focus of HR on staffing overall.

Perhaps the best way to summarize our data on HR's use of IT is to say that companies are just beginning to use it. We see a tremendous opportunity for much greater use of IT in the areas of transactional HR work. Companies already use it relatively commonly for benefit coverage and changes of address. Evidence shows that IT is being used more frequently for job information and that its effectiveness in this area is increasing. Eventually, IT systems may be widely and effectively used in the areas of advice giving and nontransactional expert support.

Currently, its use for expert advice seems to be most frequent and most effective in firms with active commitment to competency and knowledge management.

Our results suggest that the use of IT can indeed result in a shift in the focus of the HR function. It appears to be capable of shaping a new HR both by freeing up HR professionals to attend to other issues and by being an integral part of HR emphases, such as employee development and strategic support. We believe that IT applications have the potential to fundamentally change the way organizations manage and deliver HR. However, our results clearly show that this has not yet happened in most firms.

SECTION 8

eHR Systems

The 2001 survey asked a series of questions concerning the development of eHR systems and the access that employees have by way of IT to information and resources. As Table 8.1 indicates, approximately 83 percent of the companies said that they have an eHR system, slightly less than the number of companies that report using IT for at least some processes (92 percent).

The most common way companies obtained their eHR systems was from their enterprise resource planning (ERP) vendor. Two other approaches were popular: (1) buying pieces from application service provider (ASP) vendors and (2) developing their own eHR systems. These results are not surprising. Often, the easiest way to obtain an eHR system is to buy one from an ERP vendor; the vendor is typically already familiar with the company's IT systems and has a compatible eHR system. Thus, the vendor can simply add HR functionality to the system.

We found some significant differences in how firms with different organizational structures developed eHR systems. Single integrated firms are particularly likely to get their systems from their ERP vendor. This probably reflects the fact that they are more likely to have an ERP system that has integrated their business already, and thus adding on an eHR system is particularly easy. Large companies are also noticeably different in that they are particularly likely to develop systems themselves. One reason for this may be that they have resources internally to commit to the development of an eHR system. They are also much more likely to have a system than are other companies. Again, this probably reflects the resources a large company has and the economies of scale that can be gained from having an eHR system.

Table 8.2 presents results from a question we asked about what is available to employees through an employee portal. Only those companies that have an eHR system (83 percent) answered it. The items in the question clustered into two groups: (1) knowledge and market information and (2) general information. There is a substantial difference in the degree to which the two kinds of information are available. General information about the business is much more available than is knowledge and market information. The most commonly available kinds of information are executive messages to employees and open access to the Internet. Companies appear to be very willing to give employees access to the Internet and of course see portals as a major way to distribute business and executive messages.

Table 8.1. eHR System Development and Organization Structure					
	Percent Responding				
	All Companies	Single Integrated Business	Multiple Related Business	Several-Sector Businesses	Large Companies
No system	17.0	16.7	17.5	15.8	8.3
Developed it ourselves	19.0	13.9	26.3	18.4	29.2
Obtained it from our ERP vendor (for example, PeopleSoft)	37.4	50.0	33.3	28.9	33.3
Purchased most or all of it from vendors (ASPs) who provide pieces of an HR system	15.0	16.7	12.3	21.1	14.6
Hired a consulting firm to design it	4.1	0.0	3.5	10.5	4.2
Outsourced its design and operation to a consulting firm	1.4	0.0	1.8	0.0	4.2
Other	6.1	2.8	5.3	5.3	6.3

The results with respect to making knowledge and market information available to employees suggest that companies have yet to develop a great deal of focus on company knowledge management. For example, information about competitors, access to knowledge experts, and access to knowledge communities are all rated rather low in availability, with the typical response being that each is available to only some extent. This is obviously an area where organizations can develop much more comprehensive employee portals and improve their knowledge management as a result.

Forty-one percent of companies say that their system includes an eHR personal portal for employees. It is also interesting that life event–focused HR processes (for example, adding a dependent or retiring) are available to some extent in about 70 percent of the companies. Thus, companies seem to be making an effort to make eHR systems employee friendly and to allow employees to carry out more than a few basic transactions on the company's eHR system.

The relationship between portal information availability and organizational structure is shown in Table 8.3. There are some differences here. In particular, large organizations seem to make more knowledge and market information and general information available through employee portals. This difference may well reflect the extra communication challenges that large organizations face, as well as their having the wherewithal to support and use IT communication systems.

Table 8.2. Employee Portal Availability

	Percent Responding					Means
	Little or No Extent	Some Extent	Moderate Extent	Great Extent	Very Great Extent	
Knowledge and Market Information						**2.2**
Industry and competitor information	40	26	20	14	0	2.1
Access to technical knowledge and resources	19	29	20	21	10	2.7
Access to market knowledge	31	30	19	17	2	2.3
Access to knowledge experts	39	31	23	4	3	2.0
Access to knowledge communities	45	27	16	10	2	2.0
General Information						**3.0**
Company strategic and performance information	28	20	21	22	9	2.6
Executive messages to employees	11	12	24	28	25	3.5
Open access to Internet	6	9	12	31	41	3.9
A manager's tool kit	27	23	19	21	10	2.6
Life event–focused HR processes	32	24	23	12	10	2.4

We found a slight tendency for several-sector businesses to provide access to the most knowledge and market information. This is particularly noticeable when the comparison is between single integrated businesses and several-sector businesses. One possible explanation for this is that the sharing of knowledge and market information does not happen naturally through face-to-face and departmental systems when companies have multiple sectors. Consequently, several-sector businesses rely more on IT to acquire and distribute information and to enable leverage across the corporation.

Table 8.4 shows the relationship between the kind of information that is available on employee portals and the companies' strategic focuses and change initiatives. Again, the significant relationships with the change initiatives involve competency and knowledge management. An organization with a competency and knowledge management change initiative is particularly likely to make knowledge and market information available through an employee portal. This shows that the relationship

Table 8.3. Employee Portals and Organization Structure

	All Companies	Single Integrated Business	Multiple Related Business	Several-Sector Businesses	Large Companies
Knowledge and Market Information	2.2	2.0	2.1	2.5	2.3
Industry and competitor information	2.1	1.9	2.0	2.4	2.1
Access to technical knowledge and resources	2.7	2.5	2.6	3.0	2.7
Access to market knowledge	2.3	2.1	2.2	2.4	2.4
Access to knowledge experts	2.0	1.8	2.0	2.1	2.2
Access to knowledge communities	2.0	1.8	1.9	2.2	2.2
General Information	3.0	2.8	3.1	3.1	3.2
Company strategic and performance information	2.6	2.3	2.6	2.9	2.8
Executive messages to employees	3.5	3.3	3.5	3.4	3.7
Open access to Internet	3.9	3.7	4.0	3.9	3.9
A manager's tool kit	2.6	2.3	2.8	2.8	2.8
Life event–focused HR processes	2.4	2.2	2.7	2.4	2.7

Means; response scale: 1 = little or no extent; 2 = some extent; 3 = moderate extent; 4 = great extent; 5 = very great extent.

between organizations and their employees is significantly influenced by the type of change programs they are using.

Overall, our results suggest that most companies are moving toward the use of IT to perform the work of HR and to enhance employee capabilities and their understanding of the business. eHR can be a key enabler of an organization's strategy; however, in order for this to happen, sharing market and knowledge information through an employee portal needs to be much more broadly practiced. Organizations clearly have a long way to go with respect to providing employees with the kind of information that allows them both to understand the business that they are part of and the ways they can develop their skills and careers.

Perhaps the most impressive finding is that companies grant employees open access to the Internet. This allows employees a great opportunity for knowledge development and information acquisition. It also, of

Table 8.4. Relationship of Strategic Focuses and Change Initiatives to Employee Portals

	Strategic Focuses				Change Initiatives		
	Growth	Core Business	Quality & Speed	Knowledge- & Information-Based Strategies	Restructuring	Organizational Performance	Competency & Knowledge Management
Knowledge and Market Information	**.11**	**.11**	**-.08**	**.05**	**.03**	**.13**	**.21***
Industry and competitor information	.08	.05	-.11	.08	.08	.06	.15
Access to technical knowledge and resources	.05	.05	-.08	.06	.08	.11	.23**
Access to market knowledge	.07	.04	-.06	.03	.03	.17	.14
Access to knowledge experts	.09	.14	-.05	-.03	-.01	.16	.17
Access to knowledge communities	.18	.11	-.05	.09	-.05	.07	.20*
General Information	**.08**	**.15**	**-.09**	**.07**	**.10**	**.02**	**.10**
Company strategic and performance information	.04	.01	-.20*	-.04	.05	-.07	.05
Executive messages to employees	-.02	.13	-.05	.03	.13	.14	.05
Open access to Internet	.08	.29***	-.09	.04	.12	.04	-.03
A manager's tool kit	.05	.05	.02	.08	.08	.07	.19*
Life event–focused HR processes	.15	.09	-.03	.11	.02	-.09	.10

Zero order correlations: * $p \leq 0.05$; ** $p \leq 0.01$; *** $p \leq 0.001$.

course, raises many issues concerning misuse of the Internet and ways that companies should manage performance in an era of open access to the Internet.

Finally, the results show a relationship between the competency and knowledge management initiative and access to information. Once again, these results make the point that when organizations want to develop their knowledge, they use IT to aid the process.

SECTION 9

Effectiveness of eHR Systems

Because of the relative newness of eHR systems, little information is available about their effectiveness and about their impact on the effectiveness of organizations and their HR systems. In order to collect data on these two issues, we asked a question in the 2001 survey about eHR systems' effectiveness. As Table 9.1 indicates, a statistical analysis created four groups of effectiveness items.

eHR systems do not get very high performance ratings on any of the criteria. Indeed, the highest ratings are in the area of efficiency, but even the highest-rated item, speed, gets a rating just barely above the middle of the rating scale. All of the other effectiveness outcomes are rated from the middle of the scale downward. One positive note in the ratings of eHR effectiveness is that 65 percent of the respondents say that the systems do not alienate employees. This is important because some HR professionals feel that impersonal computerized services replace the human touch and cause employee alienation.

It is hardly surprising that the highest ratings come in the efficiency area, because this is an area where an eHR system should bring about short-term payoffs. Nevertheless, it is significant that we now have data confirming that the systems do, to some extent, improve HR services, reduce costs, and increase speed.

The lowest ratings come in business effectiveness, an area where eHR has the potential to make the biggest impact with respect to creating a business partner relationship with the rest of the organization. HR executives do not see these systems positively affecting organizational performance, strategic organizational change, and change management. This may in part be due to the newness of the systems and the fact that organizations are just beginning to learn how to use them as a strategic tool. Only time will tell whether eHR systems can make a positive contribution to organizational effectiveness.

Table 9.2 presents the data relating effectiveness to organizational structure. We found no strong relationship between the effectiveness of eHR systems and organizational structure. There is, however, a general trend for larger organizations to rate their eHR systems as more effective. Again, this may be because large organizations have put more resources into their eHR systems and therefore have better developed and more complete systems. This explanation is consistent with the finding that large companies provide more general information through their employee portals, including the sharing of knowledge and market

Table 9.1. eHR Effectiveness

eHR	Percent Responding					Means
	Little or No Extent	Some Extent	Moderate Extent	Great Extent	Very Great Extent	
Effectiveness	**14**	**26**	**44**	**14**	**2**	**2.6**
Employee Satisfaction						**3.0**
Satisfy your employees	20	30	37	12	1	2.4
Build employee loyalty	36	38	20	4	2	2.0
Alienate employees[1]	65	30	4	1	1	1.4
Efficiency						**2.9**
Improve HR services	9	22	31	33	5	3.0
Reduce HR transaction costs	13	27	29	21	10	2.9
Speed up HR processes	10	23	26	29	12	3.1
Reduce the number of employees in HR	25	31	26	14	4	2.4
Business Effectiveness						**2.2**
Provide new strategic information	31	37	21	11	0	2.1
Support strategic change	27	33	23	14	3	2.3
Support organizational growth	19	36	28	14	3	2.5
Integrate different HR processes (for example, training, compensation)	29	25	29	13	3	2.4
Enable the analysis of HR's impact on the business	39	29	16	13	3	2.1
Produce a balanced scorecard of HR's effectiveness	47	25	14	13	1	1.9
Enable analysis of workforce characteristics	26	29	21	18	6	2.5
Provide a competitive advantage	31	35	18	14	2	2.2

[1] Scale is reversed for inclusion in eHR employee satisfaction scale.

Table 9.2. eHR Effectiveness and Organization Structure

eHR	All Companies	Single Integrated Business	Multiple Related Business	Several-Sector Businesses	Large Companies
Effectiveness	2.6	2.4	2.8	2.6	2.8
Employee satisfaction	3.0	2.9	3.1	2.9	3.1
Efficiency	2.9	2.7	3.0	2.9	3.3
Business effectiveness	2.2	1.9	2.3	2.4	2.4

Means; response: 1 = little or no extent; 2 = some extent; 3 = moderate extent; 4 = great extent; 5 = very great extent.

information, areas that might be expected to improve organizational performance.

Table 9.3 indicates some significant relationships between eHR effectiveness and the strategic focuses. Just as we found with the effectiveness of computer service applications (see Section 7), respondents see eHR as more effective in organizations that are focused on knowledge- and information-based strategies.

All three change initiatives show a significant relationship to the business effectiveness items. The strongest relationship is between the competency and knowledge management change initiative and business effectiveness. Again, this relationship is not surprising, and it reinforces the potential usefulness of eHR systems in organizations that are focused on intellectual capital and performance capabilities. Apparently, eHR systems that contribute to business effectiveness are particularly likely

Table 9.3. Relationship of Strategic Focuses and Change Initiatives to eHR Effectiveness

eHR	Strategic Focuses				Change Initiatives		
	Growth	Core Business	Quality & Speed	Knowledge- & Information-Based Strategies	Restructuring	Organizational Performance	Competency & Knowledge Management
Effectiveness	.07	-.04	.02	.18*	.18*	-.02	.13
Employee satisfaction	-.03	-.04	.03	.22*	-.03	.03	.10
Efficiency	.16	.05	.13	.15	.22*	.10	.23*
Business effectiveness	.07	.08	.21*	.40***	.22*	.27**	.35***

Zero order correlation: * $p \leq 0.05$; ** $p \leq 0.01$; *** $p \leq 0.001$.

Table 9.4. Relationship of eHR Effectiveness to Computer System Use

eHR	Use Computer Systems for						
	Personnel Records	Job Information	Financial Transactions	Employee Training	Management Tools	Salary Planning/ Administration	Performance Management
Effectiveness	.40***	.28**	.34***	.26**	.29**	.20*	.14
Employee satisfaction	.28**	.11	.22*	-.02	.13	.07	.14
Efficiency	.43***	.25**	.34***	.31***	.31***	.20*	.15
Business effectiveness	.20*	.16	.31***	.28**	.39***	.24*	.22*

Zero order correlation: * $p \leq 0.05$; ** $p \leq 0.01$; *** $p \leq 0.001$.

to be developed when organizations have strategic focuses and change management efforts that are targeted at building the effectiveness of intellectual and human capital.

Table 9.4 shows the relationship between the effectiveness of eHR systems and the extent to which computer systems are used for the activities that were studied in Section 7. With the exception of the impact of eHR on employee satisfaction, the relationships are consistently positive. The effectiveness of eHR overall is related to greater use of computer systems for virtually all the activities. In addition, eHR efficiency is related to using systems for more activities, as is eHR business effectiveness. The relationships are particularly strong between eHR business effectiveness and the use of computer systems for financial transactions, management tools, and employee training. This is an interesting mix of transactional and competency-oriented applications.

Generally, the results suggest that respondents see eHR systems as more effective if they include more applications. The causal direction of this relationship is a bit difficult to determine. It may be that because eHR systems are seen to be effective, they are used for more activities, or it may be that a critical mass of use needs to take place in order for them to be seen as effective. Our belief is that to some degree both of these factors are operating and that what happens in most organizations is that success breeds further adoption; further adoption breeds further capability, which leads to the perception of greater value and effectiveness.

The relationship between the effectiveness of eHR systems and the effectiveness of particular computer service applications is shown in Table 9.5. As we might expect, the correlations are high and mostly significant. How effective a system is in carrying out particular trans-

Table 9.5. Relationship of eHR Effectiveness to Computer System Effectiveness							
	Computer System Effectiveness						
eHR	Personnel Records	Job Information	Financial Transactions	Employee Training	Management Tools	Salary Planning/ Administration	Performance Management
Effectiveness	.37***	.38**	.15	.11	.61***	.30**	.29**
Employee satisfaction	.34***	.36**	.11	.04	.47**	.35***	.21*
Efficiency	.42***	.26*	.23	.10	.59***	.26**	.28**
Business effectiveness	.19	.31*	.17	-.01	.38*	.21*	.23*
Zero order correlation: * $p \leq 0.05$; ** $p \leq 0.01$; *** $p \leq 0.001$.							

actions should be related to how effective an overall eHR system is. That said, a few points are worth mentioning here. One is the particularly high correlations between the effectiveness of computerized management tools for giving advice, planning, and searching for employees and the effectiveness of the overall eHR system. These systems seem to be particularly effective when they provide useful tools for managers.

The effectiveness of computer systems for personnel records, salary planning and administration, and job information are all significantly related to the measures of eHR effectiveness, making the point that it is important to create eHR systems that do the basics well. The low correlations are with financial transactions and training. Although the use of IT for these applications is strongly related to the ratings of the effectiveness of eHR, the effectiveness of these applications is not as strongly related to eHR effectiveness. It may be that simply having these applications is viewed as a positive feature but that their effectiveness is, at least at this stage of development, independent of the effectiveness of the overall system.

Table 9.6 shows the relationship of eHR system effectiveness to the degree of IT use. Clearly, a strong relationship exists here. Survey respondents rated completely integrated HRIS much higher on overall eHR effectiveness, efficiency, and business effectiveness. Less strongly related is employee satisfaction. The strong relationships to effectiveness are not surprising. Integrated systems offer the opportunity to do many more things with the eHR system and in particular to prepare analyses related to business effectiveness and strategy. For example, an integrated system can assess the practicality of business strategies by determining whether the organization has the capability to execute a

Table 9.6. Relationship of eHR Effectiveness to HR IT Use

	Little or No IT/Automation Present in the HR Function	Some HR Processes Are IT-Based/Automated	Most Processes Are IT-Based/Automated but Not Fully Integrated	Completely Integrated HR IT/Automated System
eHR	N = 8	N = 47	N = 51	N = 11
Effectiveness	1.8	2.5	2.9	3.0
Employee satisfaction	2.5	2.9	3.2	3.1
Efficiency	2.0	2.8	3.0	3.4
Business effectiveness	1.4	2.2	2.3	2.7

Means; response: 1 = little or no extent; 2 = some extent; 3 = moderate extent; 4 = great extent; 5 = very great extent.

particular strategy. It is also possible to determine the impacts of HR programs and to more effectively develop and reward employees.

Table 9.7 shows that respondents perceive eHR systems that include personal portals for employees as more effective on all dimensions. This probably reflects the fact that such systems are more accessible and may simply be more functional.

Table 9.8 shows a very strong positive relationship between the information that is available to employees through a portal and the effectiveness of the eHR system. When it comes to the effectiveness of eHR systems, the more information companies make available to employees through their IT systems, the better.

Table 9.7. eHR Effectiveness and Electronic Portal for Employees

	Personal Portal for Employees?	
	Yes	No
eHR	N = 50	N = 71
Effectiveness	3.0	2.4*
Employee satisfaction	3.3	2.8*
Efficiency	3.2	2.6*
Business effectiveness	2.5	2.1*

Means; response: 1 = little or no extent; 2 = some extent; 3 = moderate extent; 4 = great extent; 5 = very great extent.

* Significant difference: $p \leq 0.05$.

Table 9.8. Relationship of eHR Effectiveness to Information Available

eHR	Information Available	
	Knowledge & Market Information	General Information
Effectiveness	.45***	.57***
Employee satisfaction	.39***	.52***
Efficiency	.41***	.54***
Business effectiveness	.45***	.47***

Zero order correlation: * $p \leq 0.05$; ** $p \leq 0.01$; *** $p \leq 0.001$.

Table 9.9. eHR System Development and Effectiveness

	eHR System Development		
	Developed It Ourselves	Obtained from ERP vendor	Purchased from ASP
	N = 28	N = 55	N = 22
eHR			
Effectiveness	2.6	2.7	2.7
Employee satisfaction	3.0	3.0	3.0
Efficiency	2.9	3.0	2.7
Business effectiveness	2.0	2.3	2.1
Computer Systems Effective for			
Personnel records	2.6	2.7	2.5
Job information	2.2	2.2	2.2
Financial transactions	2.0	2.4	1.8
Employee training	2.1	2.2	2.2
Management tools	1.8	2.0	1.7
Salary planning/administration	2.3	2.4	2.5
Performance management	2.1	2.3	1.9

Means; response scale: 1 = little or no extent; 2 = some extent; 3 = moderate extent; 4 = great extent; 5 = very great extent.

Table 9.9 shows there are no strong relationships between the way an eHR system is developed and its effectiveness. The only significant result is that respondents perceived systems developed by ERP vendors to be more effective for financial transactions. This is not a surprise because ERP vendors typically specialize in financial transactions and would be expected to be leaders in this area.

Overall, respondents did not rate eHR systems as very effective. There are undoubtedly many reasons for this, including the fact that these systems are relatively new and companies are just beginning to learn how to use them effectively. The technology is advancing rapidly, and many companies may be experiencing the difficulties of dealing with a technology that is not well developed. The evidence here is quite clear that eHR systems are most effective when they fit the strategy and change initiatives of an organization. In particular, the systems are likely perceived to be successful in companies with knowledge- and information-based strategies and those that have competency and knowledge management initiatives.

Perhaps the most consistent finding is that the more things the eHR system can do and the more services it offers, the more effective respondents perceive it to be. Fully integrated systems are better than other systems; having a portal for employees seems to be better than not having a portal; and having a system that has a number of uses is better than having one with few uses. Finally, systems are rated highest when they carry out transactions well and provide management tools.

Creating a Strategic Human Resources Organization

SECTION 10

HR Skills

In a knowledge economy, the knowledge and skills requirements for support functions continually evolve just as they do for the firm's core business and technical units. Companies' business models are changing in order to increase the value they deliver to their customers. The business model of the HR function must also change in order for it to continue to support corporate performance. This requires the development of new capabilities for the function, as well as new knowledge and skills for HR professionals.

Skills Satisfaction

Table 10.1 shows the level of satisfaction with various skills required in today's HR function. When statistically analyzed, our satisfaction with skills items divided into three groups: organizational dynamics, HR functional, and business partner. One item, functional HR skills, did not group with any other item. After remaining relatively constant from 1995 to 1998, satisfaction with several skill areas improved significantly from 1998 to 2001. This increase is most evident with respect to organizational dynamics skills and HR functional skills.

Not surprisingly, the highest level of satisfaction is with the traditional HR functional skills, an area where respondents also report a significant increase in satisfaction. Because we evaluated these skills with one survey item, we cannot say anything about levels of satisfaction with particular areas of HR functional expertise. However, this overall increase most likely means that HR professionals have developed an increased sophistication in developing HR systems that support strategy and that they are taking a more proactive role in making these systems flexible enough to address business needs. Given the historical tendency to see the HR function as rigid and inflexible in the development and application of HR systems, a move in this direction would be an important step toward the function's becoming a more effective business partner.

The next highest levels of satisfaction are with skills that pertain to organizational dynamics, including interpersonal skills, team skills, consulting, coaching, and leadership and management skills. We found a statistically significant improvement in every one of these organizational dynamics skills. Although satisfaction with leadership and management skills and with coaching, facilitation, and consultation skills is just barely in the positive range, we find it encouraging that these skills are

Table 10.1. Satisfaction with Current Skills of the HR Staff

	Percent Responding					Means		
	Very Dissatisfied	Dissatisfied	Neutral	Satisfied	Very Satisfied	1995	1998	2001
HR Functional Skills	0	7	15	53	25	**3.7**	**3.5**	**4.0***
Organizational Dynamics						**3.2**	**3.1**	**3.6***
Team skills	0	9	25	59	7	3.3	3.2	3.7*
Consultation skills	2	15	37	39	7	3.0	2.9	3.4*
Coaching and facilitation	1	12	33	48	5	3.2	3.1	3.4*
Leadership/management skills	1	14	40	40	5	3.1	2.9	3.3*
Interpersonal skills	0	4	10	69	17	3.7	3.5	4.0*
Business Partner						—	—	**3.0**
Business understanding	0	20	35	37	9	3.0	2.9	3.3*
Strategic planning	5	30	41	20	4	—	2.8	2.9
Organizational design	3	31	45	19	2	—	2.7	2.9
Change management	2	23	37	35	3	—	—	3.2
Cross-functional experience	1	36	44	16	3	2.9	2.8	2.9
Global understanding	7	36	40	16	2	—	2.6	2.7
Administrative						—	—	**3.4**
Record keeping	0	7	29	51	13	3.6	3.6	3.7
Managing contractors/vendors	1	15	43	31	9	—	3.2	3.3
IT	4	19	42	31	4	—	—	3.1

* Significant difference ($p \leq .05$) between 1995 and 2001.

increasing. Today's HR professionals need to have these organizational dynamics skills in order to play an influential role in their organizations.

The lowest area of satisfaction is business partner skills. Business understanding shows a significant increase; however, respondents perceive skill deficits in the substantive business support areas of strategic planning and organization design, as well as in cross-functional and global understanding. Satisfaction with change management skills remains in the neutral range. Thus, although HR professionals may increasingly understand the business, our results suggest they still do not bring substantive business expertise to the table. This clearly has to change if HR is to influence strategy and be an effective business partner.

Finally, satisfaction with administrative skills is mixed. Respondents see record-keeping skills positively. However, respondents are neutral about skills in two relatively new aspects of administration: (1) management of

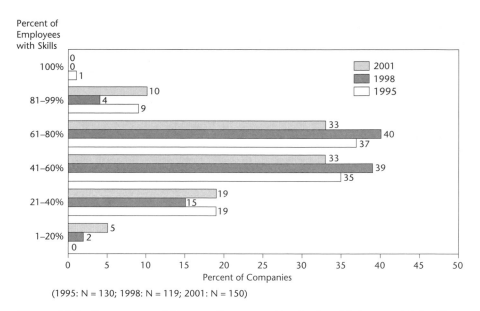

Percent of Employees with Skills

(1995: N = 130; 1998: N = 119; 2001: N = 150)

Figure 10.1. Percentage of Human Resources Professional/Managerial Staff with Necessary Skill Set

contractors and vendors and (2) IT. These skill areas have increased in importance in today's world, where outsourcing and IT-based HR administrative systems are increasingly central to carrying out the HR role.

Although satisfaction with skills in some areas has improved, Figure 10.1 indicates that the percentage of HR professionals and managers who have the necessary overall skill has not changed significantly. Apparently, respondents view the areas of skill deficit—business partner skills and management of vendors and IT—as important gaps in the overall skill portfolio of the HR function. Thus, although HR professionals have made progress in developing skills in the more traditional areas of HR expertise and organizational dynamics, many have not yet developed the full set of skills required to be a strategic partner.

We found no significant differences in satisfaction with skills among companies with different structures and between large and smaller companies. Strategy and change initiatives do make a difference, however (see Table 10.2). Satisfaction with organizational dynamics and with business partner skills is higher when companies have a quality and speed strategy. These strategies place pressures on HR for speed and quality, and they demand a more skilled set of professionals. Organizational dynamics skills are related to having organizational performance improvement initiatives in place, no doubt reflecting the teaming, facilitating, and coaching roles that HR may play in quality and speed initiatives.

The strong relationship between knowledge-based strategies and satis-

Table 10.2. Relationship of Strategic Focuses and Change Initiatives to HR Skills Satisfaction

Satisfaction	Strategic Focuses				Change Initiatives		
	Growth	Core Business	Quality & Speed	Knowledge- & Information- Based Strategies	Restructuring	Organizational Performance	Competency & Knowledge Management
HR functional skills	.07	-.14	.05	.19*	.07	.04	.10
Organizational dynamics skills	-.02	.03	.21*	.29***	.15	.23**	.32***
Business partner skills	.08	-.08	.19*	.25**	.04	.09	.28***
Administrative skills	.08	.04	.10	.25**	.04	.08	.19*

Zero order correlation: * $p \leq 0.05$; ** $p \leq 0.01$; *** $p \leq 0.001$.

faction with all four skill areas is quite striking. Closely related is the finding that having competency and knowledge management initiatives in place relates to satisfaction with organizational dynamics, business partner, and administrative skills. One interpretation of these findings is that firms with knowledge and competency strategies and initiatives also have a focus on the development of the capabilities of HR professionals. This pattern may reflect as well the success of HR functions in supporting initiatives that rely heavily on human capital. It may be that HR is stepping up to the challenge when the focus is on using human capital as a source of competitive advantage.

HR Skills and IT

If using IT to deliver traditional HR services and to expand service offerings is an integral part of the business and organizational model for HR, this should affect the skills that are needed in HR. It requires HR to develop skills in managing IT system developers, vendors, and operators. Further, if these information systems are tools for providing HR services, HR needs to embed them with expert knowledge and optimized processes. The knowledge embedded in these systems extends HR's reach and capabilities, and it may even extend the skills and knowledge of HR professionals as well as enabling self-service by managers and employees. In a transitional environment, eHR may also free up professional HR time to develop and use new value-adding skills.

Table 10.3 shows the relationship between the use of IT for various purposes and satisfaction with the skills in the HR organization. Satisfaction with administrative skills relates to the extent of use of IT for many purposes: salary planning and administration, personnel records, financial transactions, employee training, and the provision of management tools.

Table 10.3. Relationship of HR Skills Satisfaction to Use of IT

Satisfaction	Use Computer Systems for						
	Personnel Records	Job Information	Financial Transactions	Employee Training	Management Tools	Salary Planning/ Administration	Performance Management
HR functional skills	.11	.10	.17*	.01	.16	.23**	.07
Organizational dynamics skills	.09	.07	.18*	.07	.18*	.14	.06
Business partner skills	.07	-.02	.22**	.04	.17*	.09	-.08
Administrative skills	.17*	.13	.23**	.18*	.19*	.20*	.00

* Zero order correlation: * $p \le 0.05$; ** $p \le 0.01$; *** $p \le 0.001$.

Satisfaction with functional HR skills and with organizational dynamics skills relates to the use of IT for salary administration and financial transactions. Satisfaction with business partner skills relates to the use of IT for financial transactions and the provision of management tools.

The strong relationship of IT use for financial transactions to skills satisfaction in all three nontransactional areas is important. It provides evidence that such use frees up HR resources so that HR professionals can concentrate on developing and using skills in the higher value added areas of system development and expert consultation.

Table 10.4 shows the relationship of satisfaction with skills to the effectiveness of the IT service applications. The most interesting finding is that the effectiveness of IT for record keeping, performance management, and financial transactional purposes is related to satisfaction with all three areas of nontransactional HR skills: organizational dynamics, functional, and business partner skills. Again, this provides evidence that having effective systems to perform transactions supports HR professionals' skill development and the demonstration of competence in other areas. Not surprisingly, satisfaction with administrative skills is strongly related to the effectiveness of all computer applications except management tools.

Table 10.5 shows the relationship of the overall effectiveness of eHR to satisfaction with HR skills. The most striking relationship is between satisfaction with business partner skills and all aspects of eHR effectiveness. Again, we see evidence that the effective use of eHR systems may free up HR professionals for business partner activities. We also find a strong relationship between all four eHR scores and satisfaction with HR administrative skills. This finding helps establish that effective eHR systems can improve the performance of the HR organization.

Table 10.4. Relationship of HR Skills Satisfaction to Effectiveness of IT

Satisfaction	Computer Systems Effective for						
	Personnel Records	Job Information	Financial Transactions	Employee Training	Management Tools	Salary Planning/ Administration	Performance Management
HR functional skills	.22*	.04	.27*	.16	.06	.14	.22*
Organizational dynamics skills	.21*	.02	.27*	.14	.11	.08	.28**
Business partner skills	.27**	-.01	.34**	.20	.25	.15	.32***
Administrative skills	.28**	.25*	.44***	.35**	.18	.37***	.22*

* Zero order correlation: * $p \leq 0.05$; ** $p \leq 0.01$; *** $p \leq 0.001$.

Table 10.5. Relationship of HR Skills Satisfaction to eHR Effectiveness

Satisfaction	eHR Effectiveness	eHR Employee Satisfaction	eHR Efficiency	eHR Business Effectiveness
HR functional skills	.15	.16	.14	.16
Organizational dynamics skills	.14	.23*	.15	.23*
Business partner skills	.29***	.32***	.26**	.27**
Administrative skills	.31***	.30***	.19*	.21*

* Zero order correlation: * $p \leq 0.05$; ** $p \leq 0.01$; *** $p \leq 0.001$.

The relationships between the measures of eHR effectiveness and organizational dynamics skills are not strong but still interesting. Satisfaction with organizational dynamics skills relates to eHR impact on employee satisfaction. Again, we may see a substitution effect: eHR may have freed up HR employees to spend more time using and developing their teaming, coaching, facilitation, and leadership skills as they spend less time on day-to-day transactions. Thus, eHR may result not only in more efficient and effective services, it may increase the ability of HR professionals to concentrate their energies on organizational and employee capabilities and concerns.

Finally, it is striking that no significant relationships exist between satisfaction with eHR effectiveness and satisfaction with HR functional skills. This would seem to provide additional support for the notion that the major benefit of IT applications in HR is not to improve the functional capabilities of the HR organization but rather to free up HR to develop and use more business partner skills.

Conclusion

We find improvement in HR skills in the areas of administrative skills, functional expertise, and organizational dynamics. Although HR professionals significantly improved in business understanding, they do not appear to have improved their overall business partner skills. Apparently, the demand for skills, particularly in the area of business partnership, outstrips the function's ability to supply them. Overall, respondents perceived a smaller percentage of HR professionals as having the requisite skill set. Interestingly, the extent of use of IT, the effectiveness of the IT applications, and the overall effectiveness of eHR relate to satisfaction with HR skills, and in particular to skills in the business partner area.

We saw earlier that HR is taking on new roles, but it is not shedding its old roles. These data indicate that as eHR is used to provide many of the transactional and service roles that HR professionals used to provide personally, it frees the HR staff to develop skills and play higher value-added roles.

It is possible that most HR functions are in the middle of a transition to being a strategic partner. They are still getting their eHR systems in place, enhancing their functional capabilities and their ability to play process roles, and developing their business support skills. Promising signs indicate that, with high-quality IT applications, HR professionals can indeed create the focus and time to be business partners. Finally, the development and administration of IT systems has in itself created new roles for HR professionals in managing development, systems, and vendors. These are areas where HR professionals still need to enhance their skills.

SECTION 11

Effectiveness of the HR Organization

We asked respondents to judge the effectiveness of their HR organization in thirteen areas. As Table 11.1 shows, our statistical analysis produced three groups of effectiveness items. One included a wide range of HR activities, whereas the other two focused on very specific activities: managing outsourcing and operating shared services units and centers of excellence.

In 1995, 1998, and again in 2001, the effectiveness ratings are highest for providing HR services. This finding is consistent with other studies, which have found that HR tends to be rated particularly highly for the delivery of basic HR services (Csoka and Hackett, 1998). However, the ratings for HR services reach only seven on a ten-point scale. Also rated highly is being an employee advocate, another service-oriented traditional strength of many HR departments.

The HR organization is rated relatively poorly in four areas. Perhaps the two most critical ones are providing change consulting and developing business strategies. Performing well in these areas is particularly critical to HR being an effective business and strategic partner. They are areas where studies have shown that line management needs and wants help from the HR organization (Csoka and Hackett, 1998).

The ratings are also low for operating centers of excellence and shared services units, and they are relatively low for managing outsourcing of HR expertise. This is a critical failing if, as we expect, organizations are going to increase their use of outsourcing and shared services. Companies cannot derive the intended benefits from shared services, centers of excellence, or outsourcing relationships if they are poorly run. Business units are the customers of these centralized units and services, and they rely on HR to make sure these units deliver high-quality service. If this does not happen, business units will apply pressure to decentralize HR, arguing that the only way they can get the services they require is by controlling them.

Furthermore, effectively managing an important part of the HR organization is a way to establish credibility as a potential business partner. A group that cannot manage its own operations often has trouble earning credibility as an adviser and consultant to other parts of the organization that are trying to improve their effectiveness. Therefore, if HR wants to have credibility as a business partner, it needs to do a good job of managing outsourcing and shared services units. Therefore, the effective management of service units and contractors is an important HR competency.

Table 11.1. Effectiveness of HR Organization

	Means		
	1995	**1998**	**2001**
HR Effectiveness			**6.4**
Providing HR services	7.2	7.0	7.3
Providing change consulting services	5.8	5.5	5.7
Being a business partner	6.3	6.5	6.4
Developing organizational skills and capabilities	6.0	5.7	6.0
Tailoring HR practices to fit business needs	6.9	6.9	6.7
Helping shape a viable employment relationship for the future	—	5.8	6.4*
Helping to develop business strategies	—	6.2	5.8
Being an employee advocate	—	6.8	7.2
Change management	—	—	6.1
Outsourcing Effectiveness	—	**6.3**	**6.2**
Managing outsourcing of transactional services (for example, benefits)	—	6.5	6.4
Managing outsourcing of HR expertise (for example, compensation design)	—	6.2	6.0
Shared Services Effectiveness	—	**5.6**	**5.7**
Operating centers of excellence	—	5.5	5.6
Operating shared services units	—	5.7	6.0

Response scale: 1 = not meeting needs; 10 = all needs met.

* Significant difference ($p \leq .05$) between 1998 and 2001.

A comparison between the 1998 and 2001 data shows some differences. On the positive side, the respondents in 2001 rated their HR functions more highly on developing organizational skills and capabilities, helping shape a viable employment relationship for the future, being an employee advocate, and operating shared services units. These improvements are encouraging, but only one, shaping an employment relationship, is statistically significant. Further, several key effectiveness areas, including tailoring practices and being a business partner, actually show a small decline.

The results relating the effectiveness of the HR function to organizational structure appear in Table 11.2. The overall effectiveness of the HR function and its effectiveness at managing shared services are signifi-

Table 11.2. Effectiveness and Organizational Structure

	All Companies	Single Integrated Business	Multiple Related Business	Several-Sector Businesses	Large Companies
Overall effectiveness[1]	6.2	5.3	6.4	6.1*	6.2
HR effectiveness	6.4	6.1	6.5	6.3	6.5
Outsourcing effectiveness	6.2	5.6	6.7	6.1	6.3
Shared services effectiveness	5.7	4.5	6.2	5.6*	5.9

Means; response scale: 1 = not meeting needs; 10 = all needs met.
* Significant difference at $p \leq .05$.
[1] = Includes all questions.

cantly lower in single integrated businesses compared to companies with multiple related businesses and several sectors. Single integrated businesses are also lower in functional HR effectiveness and outsourcing effectiveness, although the differences are not significant.

It appears that HR does not, or perhaps does not have the opportunity to, add as much value in single integrated businesses, perhaps because the human capital and organizational challenges are less complex. HR functions in multiple related businesses, however, are the most effective in all areas. They are significantly more effective at managing shared services, and their score on managing outsourcing is noticeably higher than that of the other two groups, possibly because when businesses have similar service needs it makes it easier to achieve business leverage with common systems and services. Table 11.2 also shows that the effectiveness of HR in large companies is not perceived to be different than in all companies.

Three of the strategic focuses show relationships to the effectiveness of the HR organization (see Table 11.3). Growth is related to overall effectiveness and to HR effectiveness. A possible reason for this is that growth creates the opportunity for HR to perform well. Growth almost always involves hiring and training, activities that have historically been the strength of the HR function.

Quality and speed strategies are also related to HR effectiveness. A key issue here may be change management. Improvements in quality and speed usually require skilled change management and training. Thus, this strategy provides the opportunity for HR to develop and deliver services that can contribute to its success.

Creating a Strategic Human Resources Organization

Table 11.3. Relationship of Strategic Focuses to Change Initiatives and HR Effectiveness

	Strategic Focuses				Change Initiatives		
	Growth	Core Business	Quality & Speed	Knowledge- & Information-Based Strategies	Restructuring	Organizational Performance	Competency & Knowledge Management
Overall effectiveness[1]	.23*	.08	.14	.31**	.15	.07	.19
HR effectiveness	.19*	-.03	.20*	.33***	.07	.14	.31***
Outsourcing effectiveness	.03	.11	-.11	.09	.07	-.07	.06
Shared services effectiveness	.11	-.02	-.02	.27**	.01	.06	.14

Zero order correlation: * $p \leq 0.05$; ** $p \leq 0.01$; *** $p \leq 0.001$.

[1] = Includes all questions.

The strongest relationships with HR effectiveness clearly occur when the strategy is knowledge and information based. HR is rated as much more effective when this is a key strategy focus. Even shared services effectiveness is related to the knowledge- and information-based strategy focus. What most likely brings about this strong relationship is the important role that HR can play when a company implements a knowedge- and information-based strategy. Human capital is obviously a critical element in any knowledge- and information-based strategy, and as a result organizations that have this strategy invest more in building an effective HR organization.

The results with respect to change initiatives very much support the point that when an organization focuses on knowledge and information, HR tends to be more effective. In Table 11.3, the competency and knowledge management change initiative correlates very strongly with the rated effectiveness of the HR organization. Clearly, when intellectual capital is important to organizations, they seem to have much more effective HR functions.

We cannot provide a definitive answer to why HR is more effective when organizations are focused on information and knowledge. But we think it is because organizations that are focused on information and knowledge are more concerned with their human capital. This in turn leads to them developing first-rate HR organizations. It also provides the HR organization with a chance to make a major contribution to organizational effectiveness.

Overall, the data on effectiveness present a mixed picture of the HR function. Of particular concern are the relatively low scores in effectiveness areas that are related to performing as a business partner. Also on the negative side is the lack of any general increase in the effectiveness of the HR organization from 1995 to 2001. Granted, the number of areas where HR needs to be effective has increased, as have the standards for evaluation. Nevertheless, the absolute scores make clear that respondents view HR as much less effective than it can be.

On the positive side are the relationships of companies' strategies and change initiatives with HR effectiveness. These data strongly suggest that when organizations particularly focus on knowledge and competency activities, the HR function is more effective. This argues well for the long-term future of the HR function because organizations are increasingly likely to be in knowledge-based work and therefore place a major strategic focus on knowledge and competency development. In essence, what these data suggest is that the door may be opening for HR to be more effective if it can deliver the kinds of services that the knowledge economy needs.

Creating a Strategic Human Resources Organization

SECTION 12

Determinants of HR Effectiveness

What determines how effective an HR organization is? To answer this question, we need to look at the relationship between the rated effectiveness of the HR organization and the practices and activities that are likely to influence effectiveness.

Table 12.1 shows the relationship between the way the HR function is organized and its rated effectiveness. Many of these are significant, indicating that the organization of the HR function affects its effectiveness.

The strongest relationship with effectiveness concerns the use of corporate centers of excellence, centralized processing, rotation of people within HR, and self-service. Also significantly associated with effectiveness are the outsourcing of transactional (but not expert) services, development of HR systems through joint line-HR task forces, activities being done by line managers, and self-funding for HR services.

A major surprise in the findings concerns decentralization. We expected that having HR generalists support business units would be strongly related to effectiveness, but the results do not support this. Although it is in the expected direction, even the item in the decentralization group on having a very small corporate staff is not significantly related to effectiveness (see Table 12.1). One possible explanation is that the ratings of effectiveness are coming from senior corporate HR executives, and they may not be particularly comfortable with having resources in business units. As a result, they may see their HR organization as less effective than it would be if everybody were in a centralized corporate unit. Nevertheless, organizations do not appear to be abandoning this practice, and it seems difficult to imagine the HR function being a business partner without achieving partnerships in each business unit.

Overall, the results concerning the organization of HR very much support our view of what HR must do to be effective in today's business environment. Specifically, HR must handle the transaction work efficiently, while at the same time supporting the business units with excellent HR knowledge and well-trained HR employees. The results also support the view that HR systems are best developed with input from the line organization. If members of the line organization are going to engage in self-service, then it makes particular sense to get them involved in the development of the systems so that they will be committed to their effective operation.

Table 12.1. Relationship of HR Organization to HR Effectiveness

	HR Effectiveness
Outsourcing	**.26***
Transactional work is outsourced.	.31**
Areas of HR expertise are outsourced.	.12
HR Service Teams	**.35***
HR teams provide service and support the business.	.12
Corporate centers of excellence.	.36***
HR systems and policies developed through joint line-HR task teams.	.28**
Decentralization	**.10**
Decentralized HR generalists support business units.	.11
Very small corporate staff—most HR managers and professionals are out in businesses.	.18
HR practices vary across business units.	-.06
Resource Efficiency	**.43***
Administrative processing is centralized.	.36***
Self-funding requirements exist for HR services.	.24*
Some activities that used to be done by HR are now done by line managers.	.30**
Some transactional activities that used to be done by HR are done by employees on a self-service basis.	.37***
Rotation	**.31**
People rotate within HR.	.42***
People rotate into HR.	.13
People rotate out of HR to other functions.	.16

Zero order correlation: * $p \leq 0.05$; ** $p \leq 0.01$; *** $p \leq 0.001$.

Table 12.2 shows the relationship between the type of business strategy partnership that the HR organization has and its effectiveness. For this analysis, we divided the business strategy relationships into two categories so that each HR function was characterized as either a full partner or not a full partner. The results for these two groups are significantly different on most of the measures of HR effectiveness. The effectiveness items with the largest differences are those concerned with business strategy, change management, organizational development, and future employment relationships.

The result with respect to business strategy is not surprising; the data simply confirm that HR is most effective in developing strategy when it is a full partner. More interesting are the results concerning managing change, developing capabilities, and tailoring HR practices. They sug-

Creating a Strategic Human Resources Organization

Table 12.2. Relationship of Type of Strategic Partner to HR Effectiveness		
	Means	
	Not Full Partner	**Full Partner**
Number of respondents	86	60
Overall Effectiveness	**5.9**	**6.5***
HR Effectiveness	**6.0**	**6.8***
Providing HR services	7.2	7.5
Providing change consulting services	5.4	6.1*
Being a business partner	6.0	6.9*
Developing organizational skills and capabilities	5.5	6.5*
Tailoring HR practices to fit business needs	6.4	7.0*
Helping shape a viable employment relationship for the future	6.0	6.9*
Helping to develop business strategies	5.2	6.6*
Being an employee advocate	7.0	7.5
Change management	5.7	6.5*
Outsourcing Effectiveness	**6.1**	**6.4**
Managing outsourcing of transactional services (for example, benefits)	6.3	6.7
Managing outsourcing of HR expertise (for example, compensation design)	5.9	6.1
Shared Services Effectiveness	**5.7**	**5.8**
Operating centers of excellence	5.5	5.8
Operating shared service units	6.1	6.0

* Significant difference ($p \leq .05$) between the two categories.

Response scale: 1 = not meeting needs; 10 = all needs met.

gest that making HR a full strategic partner enables the HR staff to better support more strategy implementation. This interpretation of the results makes sense. HR executives who understand the business strategy most likely can do a better job of supporting the strategy. In addition, they may even influence it so that it is more realistic in terms of the organization's and HR's ability to execute it. However, we must point out that this is simply a relationship and that the causal direction between effectiveness and being a strategic partner may operate in the reverse direction. That is, HR effectiveness may be something an HR organization has to achieve in order to be regarded as a full strategic partner. Our belief is that both directions of causation most likely are operating in this particular case.

Earlier, we noted that HR organizations are spending less time maintaining records and more time being strategic business partners. Table 12.3 shows the relationship between the areas in which HR staff spend time and the effectiveness of the HR organization. The data strongly supports the idea that in order to be effective, the HR organization must decrease the amount of time spent maintaining records, auditing, and controlling and increase the amount of time spent as a strategic business partner. A negative relationship exists between time spent on records and overall effectiveness; however, a strong positive relationship exists between the degree to which an HR organization spends its time as a strategic business partner and its perceived effectiveness on many dimensions. These findings are consistent with the work of Brockbank (1999), which found that performance is higher when HR departments focus more on strategy.

Note that there is no relationship between outsourcing effectiveness and time spent as a business partner, nor is there one between shared services effectiveness and time spent as a business partner. Earlier, we argued that effectiveness in these areas is largely a matter of operational, not strategic, excellence. Thus, it is not surprising that they are not related to time spent as a strategic partner.

Although our results do not prove that spending more time being a strategic business partner and less time maintaining records leads to effectiveness, they clearly suggest that this is what happens. This conclusion is reinforced by the areas of HR performance where effectiveness is most strongly related to being a strategic business partner. The correlations are highest for helping develop business strategies, providing change-consulting services, shaping an employment relationship, and being a business partner.

Table 12.4 presents the data on the relationship between overall HR effectiveness and the degree to which HR functions have increased their attention to certain activities. It shows few significant relationships. This is surprising because our 1998 study indicated a number of significant relationships. In particular, increasing the amount of activity in the area of strategic planning, organizational design, organizational development, and HR planning were all significantly related to high ratings on effectiveness. In the present study, none of these is significantly related to effectiveness, although several are close. The reason for this is not clear, but we must remember one thing: these are ratings of activity increases, not levels of activity. Thus, the lack of a significant relationship does not negate the finding that HR organizations focusing more on strategic business partnering are more effective.

Creating a Strategic Human Resources Organization

Table 12.3. Relationship of HR Role to Effectiveness

	Maintaining Records	Auditing/ Controlling	Providing HR Services	Developing HR Systems	Strategic Business Partnering
Overall Effectiveness	**-.23***	**-.19**	**-.09**	**.03**	**.29****
HR Effectiveness	**-.15**	**-.11**	**-.16**	**-.03**	**.32*****
Providing HR services	-.23**	-.02	.04	-.11	.17*
Providing change consulting services	-.19*	-.06	-.15	.03	.28***
Being a business partner	-.15	-.11	-.17*	-.08	.35***
Developing organizational skills and capabilities	-.08	-.03	-.19*	.01	.24**
Tailoring HR practices to fit business needs	-.15	-.12	.01	-.01	.13
Helping shape a viable employment relationship for the future	-.20*	-.12	-.12	.04	.28***
Helping to develop business strategies	-.00	-.18*	-.29***	.00	.37***
Being an employee advocate	-.07	-.10	-.08	-.04	.19*
Change management	-.12	-.05	-.18*	-.04	.30***
Outsourcing Effectiveness	**-.11**	**-.15**	**-.10**	**.15**	**.14**
Managing outsourcing of transactional services (for example, benefits)	-.04	-.13	-.09	.06	.13
Managing outsourcing of HR expertise (for example, compensation design)	-.14	-.12	-.08	.16	.13
Shared Services Effectiveness	**-.13**	**-.15**	**.01**	**-.01**	**.14**
Operating centers of excellence	-.16	-.11	-.01	-.05	.18
Operating shared services units	-.08	-.14	-.02	.03	.11

Zero order correlation: * $p \leq 0.05$; ** $p \leq 0.01$; *** $p \leq 0.001$.

One way to judge the impact of IT on the effectiveness of the HR organization is by the relationship between the degree of IT use and HR effectiveness. Table 12.5 shows the average overall performance rating of HR effectiveness for the five different degrees of HR IT use. It shows a relatively clear-cut relationship in the direction of more use of IT being associated with greater effectiveness. This, of course, is only a relationship. It does not prove a causal direction, but it suggests that IT can improve the effectiveness of the HR organization.

Table 12.4. Relationship of HR Activity Changes to HR Effectiveness	
	HR Effectiveness
Design and Organizational Development	**.18**
HR planning	.15
Organizational development	.18
Organizational design	.12
Strategic planning	.10
Compensation and Benefits	**.28****
Compensation	.38***
Benefits	.12
Legal and Regulatory	**.07**
Employee record keeping	-.05
Legal affairs	-.04
Affirmative action	.08
Employee assistance	.22*
Employee Development	**.11**
Employee training/education	.10
Management development	.13
Performance appraisal	-.02
Career planning	.09
Competency/talent assessment	.15
Recruitment and Selection	**.07**
Recruitment	.03
Selection	.09
HRIS	**.08**
Union Relations	**-.06**
Zero order correlation: * $p \leq 0.05$; ** $p \leq 0.01$; *** $p \leq 0.001$.	

Table 12.6 further examines the relationship between the use of computer systems for different activities and HR effectiveness. A number of significant relationships are apparent here, all of which are in the direction of greater computer use leading to the HR function being seen as more effective. The strongest relationship involves the use of the system to search for employees with specific skills and competencies. This is part of a group of management tools that, as a whole, show a strong relationship to HR effectiveness. The relationship of the management tool group to effectiveness quite clearly makes the point that eHR is most effective when it enables managers to do their jobs better.

Table 12.5. Relationship of IT Use to HR Effectiveness	
	Mean Effectiveness Rating
Completely integrated HR IT system	6.6
Most processes are IT-based but not fully integrated	6.5
Some HR processes are IT-based	6.0
Little IT present in HR function	4.6
No IT present	5.6
Means; response scale: 1 = not meeting needs; 10 = all needs met.	

Table 12.6. Relationship of Computer Systems Use to HR Effectiveness	
Use Computer Systems for	HR Effectiveness
Personnel Records	**.17**
Change benefit coverage	.12
Change address and/or other personal information	.21*
Job Information	**.19**
Apply for a job (external applicants)	.16
Apply for a job (internal applicants)	.18
Post job openings	.17
Post personal résumé/bio	.06
Financial Transactions	**.26***
Travel and expense reimbursements	.23*
Purchase products and services from vendors	.20
Employee Training	**.11**
New-hire orientation	.24*
Technical skills training	.00
Scheduling training and development	.03
Management Tools	**.29****
Career development planning	.11
Obtain advice and information on handling personnel issues	.16
Identifying management development resources	.21*
Management development training	.16
Search for employees with specified skills/competencies	.35***
Salary Planning/Administration	**.33***
Performance Management	**.05**
Zero order correlation: * $p \leq 0.05$; ** $p \leq 0.01$; *** $p \leq 0.001$.	

The use of computer systems for salary administration is also significantly correlated with effectiveness. This is not surprising. Salary administration is a key HR area because it affects the attraction, retention, and motivation of employees. However, managers often feel that HR unnecessarily constrains their salary decisions and that salary administration is tedious and difficult. As a consequence, salary administration often frustrates managers and causes them to have a low opinion of the HR function. Putting salary administration on an eHR system can do a considerable amount to make the process more efficient and effective and to give managers increased ownership and control.

Other IT applications that improve HR effectiveness include the ability to change personal information and carry out various financial transactions without time-consuming paperwork processes. Providing new-hire orientation information on the computer is a way to save time as well as provide a high-quality presentation of information about the company. It can also allow employees an easy way to provide personal information and sign up for benefits.

The availability of information through a portal is strongly related to the effectiveness of the HR function (see Table 12.7). The availability of knowledge and market information and of general information are highly correlated with HR effectiveness. Interestingly, the highest single correlation is with a manager's tool kit. The more managerial tools are available, the more effective the HR function is perceived to be. Of course, these are correlational data and do not establish causality. Nevertheless, we believe that it is reasonable to assume that when HR plays a role in providing tools and information that help employees do their jobs and manage their careers, it leads to HR being more effective. In addition, HR systems themselves may very well work much more effectively when good information about the systems and the organization is provided to employees. For example, performance management processes and incentive systems may operate better in an environment where employees are well informed about company strategy and operating results.

Better skills lead to a more effective HR organization, hardly a surprising point! What is interesting about the data in Table 12.8, however, is the kind of skills that are most strongly related to HR effectiveness: business and organizational dynamics skills. The more skilled the employees in the HR function are in working with others, being team members, coaching, consulting, and leading, the more effective the HR function is. In other words, HR effectiveness relates to the ability of HR professionals to influence the effectiveness of others. Further, the more the HR organization staff understands the business and participates in

Creating a Strategic Human Resources Organization

Table 12.7. Relationship of Employee Portal Information to HR Effectiveness

	HR Effectiveness
Knowledge and Market Information	**.39***
Industry and competitor information	.31**
Access to technical knowledge and resources	.36***
Access to market knowledge	.38***
Access to knowledge experts	.28**
Access to knowledge communities	.29**
General Information	**.47***
Company strategic and performance information	.34**
Executive messages to employees	.23*
Open access to Internet	.28**
A manager's tool kit	.50***
Life event–focused HR processes	.36***

Zero order correlation: * $p \leq 0.05$; ** $p \leq 0.01$; *** $p \leq 0.001$.

strategic design and change management, the more effective the HR organization. This finding is very consistent with many of our earlier findings. It shows once again that if HR wants to be effective, it needs to be a player in the business. This means having the skills to contribute to its success and helping the organization perform more effectively.

In Section 1, we reported that 25 percent of the heads of HR organizations do not have HR backgrounds. This raises the important question whether it makes a difference in the performance of the HR organization. Table 12.9 provides data relevant to this question. It compares the effectiveness of HR organizations headed by people with and without backgrounds in HR management. Although we found no significant differences in effectiveness, some interesting patterns emerge.

Overall, the organizations headed by people with HR backgrounds get slightly higher ratings. Those organizations headed by individuals with HR backgrounds score higher on providing change management services, developing organizational skills and capabilities, and helping to develop business strategy. As has already been found, these are key performance areas with respect to HR becoming a strategic business partner. Thus, it appears that an HR organization headed by an individual with an HR background may be better positioned to be a strategic partner and contribute to the effectiveness of the company. The only area where leaders without HR backgrounds appear to do better is

Table 12.8. Relationship of Staff Skills to HR Effectiveness	
	HR Effectiveness
HR Functional Skills Satisfaction	**.44***
Organizational Dynamics Skills	**.69***
Team skills	.47***
Consultation skills	.40***
Coaching and facilitation	.54***
Leadership/management skills	.54***
Interpersonal skills	.50***
Business Partner Skills Satisfaction	**.69***
Business understanding	.53***
Strategic planning	.54***
Organizational design	.49***
Change management	.69***
Cross-functional experience	.37***
Global understanding	.48***
Administrative Skills Satisfaction	**.47***
Record keeping	.13
Managing contractors/vendors	.49***
IT	.37***

Zero order correlations: * $p \leq 0.05$; ** $p \leq 0.01$; *** $p \leq 0.001$.

Means; response scale: 1 = not meeting needs; 10 = all needs met.

managing shared services units, an area relying to a great extent on operational management skills.

Why are HR organizations that are headed by individuals with an HR management background more effective? One explanation is that an organization may appoint an individual from outside HR to head the HR function when it is in trouble and performing poorly. Thus, the background of the head of the HR organization may reflect more on the organization's past performance than on the effectiveness of its current leadership. Another explanation is that individuals with an HR background simply have the deep and broad HR knowledge and skills required to lead the development and implementation of sound HR strategies, as well as to lead an organization composed of HR professionals. Particularly if they have an understanding of the business, they would seem to be in a much better position to combine management of the HR function with being a strategic partner.

Table 12.9. HR Effectiveness and Background of HR Head	Background of Current Head of HR	
	HR Management	Other
Number of respondents	113	37
Overall Effectiveness	**6.2**	**6.0**
HR Effectiveness	**6.4**	**6.2**
Providing HR services	7.3	7.4
Providing change consulting services	5.8	5.5
Being a business partner	6.4	6.4
Developing organizational skills and capabilities	6.1	5.7
Tailoring HR practices to fit business needs	6.7	6.5
Helping shape a viable employment relationship for the future	6.4	6.5
Helping to develop business strategies	5.9	5.4
Being an employee advocate	7.2	7.1
Change management	6.2	5.7
Outsourcing Effectiveness	**6.2**	**6.2**
Managing outsourcing of transactional services (for example, benefits)	6.5	6.2
Managing outsourcing of HR expertise (for example, compensation design)	5.9	6.2
Shared Services Effectiveness	**5.7**	**6.0**
Operating centers of excellence	5.5	6.0
Operating shared services units	6.0	6.2

No significant differences ($p \leq .05$) between the two categories.

Overall, the survey results show relatively strong relationships between how the HR organization operates and its effectiveness. Focusing on strategy, organization design and development, employee competency development, and organizational change has high payoffs for the HR organization. Outsourcing transactional work and creating shared services units appears to lead to a more effective HR organization. We found consistently strong relationships between using IT for HR tasks and HR effectiveness. Finally, HR functions that are strategic business partners are more effective than those that are not. In Section 13, we will explore the factors that lead to HR being a strategic partner.

SECTION 13

HR as a Strategic Partner

Being a strategic partner is clearly related to the effectiveness of the HR function. But what does it take to make HR a strategic partner? How should HR be structured? What should HR focus on? How should it be staffed? In order to answer these questions, we will focus in this section on how the design and operation of the HR function is related to HR being a strategic partner.

Table 13.1 shows the relationship between HR being a strategic partner and the background of the head of HR. The results show that HR is more likely to be a full strategic partner when the head of HR has an HR background. This is a bit surprising because one might expect that having someone who is not an HR person, typically someone from the line organization, would lead to HR being more of a strategic partner. But as was true with organizational effectiveness, having someone with an HR background manage the HR function is in fact a positive when it comes to HR being a strategic partner. This raises the question: Why?

It may be that when HR is not a strategic partner in an organization, the company puts someone from outside HR in charge of the function in order to make it a strategic partner. As a result, we find that HR functions headed by people without HR backgrounds are less likely to be strategic partners. Or it may be that managers with an HR background are better at representing HR issues in the strategic partnership dialogue; hence, when they head HR, it is more likely to be a strategic partner because they bring more to the table.

Providing strategic HR knowledge and insight is an important responsibility in the knowledge economy, as well as a challenging one. Being a good strategic partner takes understanding the business, but it also takes understanding the HR function. Thus, it is quite likely that an HR head without an HR background may not be able to understand the HR issues well enough to make the function a true strategic partner with the business.

The relationship between HR organizational approaches and the degree to which HR is a strategic partner is shown in Table 13.2. With the exception of the use of outsourcing and decentralization, the items in this table are all related to the degree to which HR is a business partner. As we might expect, having service teams that operate centrally improves the likelihood that HR will be a full partner, as does decentralization. A significant relationship also exists between rotating staff into and within HR and being a full strategic partner. Rotation is a way to give people

Creating a Strategic Human Resources Organization

Table 13.1. Strategic Partner and Background of HR Head

	Percent Responding			
	No Role	Implementation Role	Input Role	Full Partner
HR management	3.6	10.0	41.8	44.5
Other	2.8	16.7	50.0	30.6

Table 13.2. Strategic Partner and HR Organizational Approaches

	No Role	Implementation Role	Input Role	Full Partner
Outsourcing	2.1	1.9	2.1	2.3
HR service teams	2.3	3.1	3.2	3.5*
Decentralization	2.9	2.8	3.1	3.4
Resource efficiency	2.6	2.3	2.5	2.8*
Rotation	1.5	1.8	2.1	2.4*

Means; response scale: 1 = little or no extent; 2 = some extent; 3 = moderate extent; 4 = great extent; 5 = very great extent.

* Significant difference ($p \leq .05$) among roles.

the insights necessary to operate as a strategic partner and, indeed, can lead to a situation where individuals from the line organization understand HR and know how to involve it in a strategic partner relationship. The relationship of decentralization is not quite statistically significant, but it is in the expected direction, most likely because it puts an HR generalist in position to be a strategic partner.

Table 13.3 shows the results concerning strategic focuses and change initiatives. Two of the four strategic focuses are clearly related to the degree to which HR is a full partner; the other two are not significantly related. The difference between HR having no role in strategy and its being a full partner is particularly large in the case of quality and speed and knowledge- and information-based strategies. As we have observed throughout the book, when knowledge and information is a key strategy, HR is particularly well positioned to contribute value at the strategic level.

The results for the change initiatives show that the competency and knowledge management initiative is significantly related to the degree to which HR is a full partner. Again, the results are consistent with the view that when the focus of an organization is on its ability to perform

Table 13.3. Strategic Partner and Strategic Focuses and Change Initiatives

	No Role	Implementation Role	Input Role	Full Partner
Strategic Focuses				
Growth	2.5	2.3	2.9	3.0
Core business	2.0	2.8	2.4	2.6
Quality and speed	2.9	3.3	3.7	3.8*
Knowledge- and information-based strategies	2.9	3.6	3.7	3.8*
Change Initiatives				
Restructuring	3.7	3.4	3.2	3.4
Organizational performance	2.1	2.9	2.9	3.1
Competency and knowledge management	1.9	2.6	2.8	3.3*

Means; response scale: 1 = little or no extent; 2 = some extent; 3 = moderate extent; 4 = great extent; 5 = very great extent.

* Significant difference ($p \leq .05$) among roles.

Table 13.4. Strategic Partner and HRIS

	Percent Responding			
	No Role	Implementation Role	Input Role	Full Partner
Completely integrated HRIS	9.1	9.1	27.3	54.5
Most processes automated but not fully integrated	1.9	11.5	50.0	36.5
Some HR processes automated	0	11.9	43.3	44.8
Little automation present in HR function	22.2	11.1	33.3	33.3
No automation present	0	50.0	50.0	0

and manage knowledge, HR is in a particularly good position to be a strategic partner.

IT represents a way to free up the HR function so that it can be a strategic partner and deliver greater value. It also makes available to HR a great deal of HR and business information; these data, which address many strategic issues, can allow it to operate as a strategic partner. We would expect, therefore, that the more HR uses information systems, the more likely it is to be a full strategic partner. Table 13.4 shows that this is in fact true. Where HR has a completely integrated information system, HR is a full partner in 54.5 percent of the companies. Where it does not, HR is not as likely to be a full partner.

Table 13.5. Strategic Partner and HR Activity Changes				
	No Role	Implementation Role	Input Role	Full Partner
Design and organizational development	3.0	3.6	3.7	4.1*
Compensation and benefits	3.8	4.0	3.7	3.7
Legal and regulatory	3.1	3.0	3.1	3.1
Employee development	3.0	3.4	3.6	3.8*
Recruitment and selection	3.3	3.5	3.7	3.9
HRIS	4.0	4.2	4.0	4.0
Union relations	3.4	2.5	2.8	2.5

Scale response: 1 = greatly decreased; 3 = stayed the same; 5 = greatly increased.

* Significant difference ($p \leq .05$) among roles.

The use of outsourcing and shared services was not related to the degree to which HR is a strategic partner. As we mention throughout the book, these approaches relate to operational excellence, not strategic business partnership. Thus, this result is not surprising.

Table 13.5 shows the relationship between the degree to which HR is a strategic partner and changes in HR activity. The results here are quite strong for several of the activity changes. On the negative side, greater attention to union relations decreases the degree to which HR is a strategic partner. In some ways, this is not surprising: union relations are a difficult and time-consuming issue in many organizations, and they may detract from HR's focus on and credibility in contributing to business strategy. By association, an HR organization that is heavily involved in managing the relationship with the union may be seen as blocking change.

Increasing activities in the areas of organizational design and development, employee development, and to a lesser degree recruitment and selection is clearly related to HR being a strategic partner. These are all areas of expertise and practice where HR can add considerable value when it is involved in strategic planning with the line organization. Thus, it is hardly surprising that a greater focus on these areas is associated with HR being a strategic partner.

A good guess as to why a relationship exists between activity changes and being a strategic partner is that the HR organization gets invited to be a strategic partner because it is competent in these areas and able to add value. Once it shows it can add value, HR becomes a true strategic

Table 13.6. Strategic Partner and HR Staff Skills

	No Role	Implementation Role	Input Role	Full Partner
HR functional skills satisfaction	3.8	3.6	4.0	4.0
Organizational dynamics skills satisfaction	3.5	3.2	3.5	3.7*
Business skills satisfaction	2.9	2.5	2.9	3.1*
Administrative skills satisfaction	3.3	3.3	3.4	3.5

Means; response scale: 1 = very dissatisfied, 2 = dissatisfied, 3 = neutral, 4 = satisfied, 5 = very satisfied.

* Significant difference ($p \leq .05$) among roles.

partner. The data on the relationship between HR being a strategic partner and the skills of HR employees supports this interpretation. As the data in Table 13.6 show, HR is more likely to have a full partner relationship when it has skills in two areas: organizational dynamics and business partnering. This supports the argument that, in order to be a strategic partner, HR needs business skills and organizational design skills.

Overall, the data present a rather clear picture of when HR is likely to be a full strategic partner. First, this occurs when HR has a structure that supports its being a strategic partner. This means rotating people, using teams, and decentralizing operations. Second, it helps to have a head of HR who has an HR management background. HR is more likely to be a strategic partner when the strategies and change initiatives in the company require the support that the HR function can deliver. There is also a clear relationship between HR's use of IT and its becoming a full strategic partner. Completely integrated HRIS helps create a strategic partnership. Finally, the skills and the effectiveness of an HR organization clearly come into play. Having the right skills helps HR become a strategic partner.

CONCLUSION   Most HR professionals agree that the HR function needs to be a strategic partner, and HR executives are focusing on and thinking of new ways of adding value. But is the HR function changing? Our study provides the best data available to answer this question.

Whereas other studies have asked about the importance of new directions and skills, our study focuses on practice and how it has changed from 1995 to 2001. It examines change by measuring the use of practices at three points in time. Other studies have asked individuals to report on the amount and kind of change that has occurred. Reports of change, because they are influenced by memory and other factors, are generally less valid than comparisons of data collected at two or more points in time. This was demonstrated in our study. Executives report a significant shift in the way HR time is being spent. However, when we compare executive reports from 1995, 1998, and 2001 on how time is spent, the percentages have not shifted. Thus, when researchers examine changes in practice by using reports of practice from different time periods, they obtain much better evidence about the kind and amount of change that has occurred.

A comparison of the results from our 1995, 1998, and 2001 surveys establishes that some change is taking place in the HR function and that changes are in the direction of its becoming more of a business and strategic partner. A number of significant changes have occurred in how HR functions are organized and how they deliver services. The most important are the following:

- HR is more likely to use service teams to support and serve business units.

- HR is more likely to have decentralized HR generalists who support business units.

- HR is paying increasing attention to recruitment and selection and less attention to union relations and benefits management. It is paying increased attention to employee development, HRIS, and organizational design and development, although the rate of increase in attention in these areas has declined over the course of the six-year study.

- The use of outsourcing for training, HRIS, benefits compensation, legal affairs, and affirmative action has increased.

- Employees and managers are increasingly serving themselves with Web-enabled systems that provide job information and performance management capabilities.

- HR executives report greater satisfaction with the HR functional skills and the organizational dynamics skills of the HR staff.

- HR is increasingly effective in helping shape a viable employment relationship for the future.

A comparison of the 1995, 1998, and 2001 results shows clearly that a number of things have not changed. Among the major areas that show no change are the following:

- The extent to which HR is a full partner in shaping business strategy

- The ratio of HR employees to total number of employees

- The amount of time spent on various HR activities

- The rotation of individuals into, out of, and within HR

- The use and effectiveness of shared services

- The problems that occur with outsourcing

- The use of outsourcing for organizational development, employee assistance, and HR planning

- The business partner skills of members of the HR organization

- The overall effectiveness of the HR organization and its effectiveness in managing shared services, outsourcing, and a number of individual areas of HR effectiveness

Overall, we found that more things stayed the same than changed when we compared our data from the three surveys. Although many of the changes we did find are significant and important, the amount of change is surprisingly small. Given the tremendous amount of attention that has been given to the importance of HR being more of a value-added function, becoming a business and strategic partner, and adding value in a number of new ways, we frankly expected much more change. We particularly expected more change from 1998 to 2001, given the change from the boom times of the late 1990s to the more difficult economic times that began in late 2000 and the many challenges that organizations have faced because of the economic slowdown. It appears that somehow the HR organization has managed to maintain a relatively stable orientation despite the amount of change going on around it. This raises a critical question: Are particular organizational conditions associated with the HR function changing?

Conditions Favoring Change

Let's look first at the issue of where the HR function is structured and acting differently. Our study found a strong relationship between what is happening in the HR function and the company's business strategy and change initiatives. Particularly important was the degree to which organizations had knowledge- and information-based strategies and change initiatives related to competency and knowledge management. To a lesser extent, the same was true of companies with strategies and initiatives focusing on organizational performance competencies such as speed and quality.

On the other hand, in companies with strategies and initiatives focused on growth, business portfolio changes such as focusing on core businesses, and restructuring, the HR function was less likely to be a strategic partner. For example, companies that report HR is a full partner, or at least has an input role to business strategy, have a greater emphasis on knowledge- and information-based strategies than on growth or portfolio-restructuring strategies. Companies that report HR has no role in strategy are more likely to have restructuring initiatives than performance improvement and competency and knowledge initiatives.

Tables C-1 and C-2 show the areas in which having knowledge-based strategies and knowledge management and competency initiatives make it more likely that the HR function operates in ways compatible with adding more value to the business and is more effective in doing so. Generally speaking, an emphasis on knowledge, competencies, and human capital appears to create a much more favorable situation for the HR function because it places a premium on acquiring, developing, using, and retaining talent.

One interesting theme in the results is that an emphasis on knowledge and competencies is associated with the use and effectiveness of eHR and especially with providing knowledge and management tools through it. This emphasis on eHR is compatible with current understandings of knowledge management that stress that IT is a powerful tool for making knowledge available through the organization (Davenport and Prusak, 1998). Knowledge can be embedded in tools that extend the knowledge workers' capabilities (Leonard-Barton, 1995), including not only the tools that employees and managers in general use but also those that HR uses. Knowledge and competency emphases are also associated with more interpersonal aspects of HR, such as the use of service teams and organizational dynamics skills. This also fits with the current understanding that IT is insufficient for delivering knowledge because the application of knowledge to solve complex and uncertain problems often requires interpersonal exchange in which people with various knowledge bases work together (Mohrman, Finegold, and Klein, forthcoming).

The results in Tables C-1 and C-2 show two important relationships. First, strategies and initiatives that focus on performance capabilities relate to many of the same features of the HR organization as knowledge

Table C-1. Significant Relationships of Strategy and Change Initiatives to HR Features

	Quality & Speed Strategy	Knowledge- & Information-Based Strategy	Knowledge & Competency Initiatives	Performance Improvement Initiatives
Time spent on strategic business partner role	✓		✓	
Use of service teams	✓	✓	✓	✓
Increased focus on recruitment			✓	
Increased focus on organization design and development	✓		✓	✓
Increased focus on employee development	✓	✓	✓	✓
Extent to which a talent strategy is in place	✓	✓	✓	✓
High potential development initiatives			✓	✓
Greater outsourcing of organization design and development				✓
More effective use of shared services		✓		
Greater satisfaction with HR functional skills		✓		
Greater satisfaction with HR organization dynamics skills	✓	✓	✓	✓
Greater satisfaction with HR business partner skills	✓	✓	✓	
Greater satisfaction with HR administrative skills	✓	✓		
Greater overall HR effectiveness		✓		
Greater satisfaction with HR functional effectiveness	✓	✓	✓	
Time spent on strategic business partner role	✓		✓	

✓ indicates a statistically significant relationship.

Table C-2. Significant Relationships of Strategy and Change Initiatives to eHR

	Quality & Speed Strategy	Knowledge- & Information-Based Strategy	Knowledge & Competency Initiatives	Performance Improvement Initiatives
Effectiveness of overall eHR		✓		
Positive impact of eHR on employee satisfaction		✓		
Positive impact of eHR on business effectiveness	✓	✓	✓	✓
Positive impact of eHR on efficiency			✓	
Management tools available electronically and seen as more effective			✓	
More market and competitive information available through employee portal			✓	

✓ indicates a statistically significant relationship.

and competency emphases. In fact, all four of the strategy and initiative areas are associated with greater use of service teams, the extent to which a talent strategy is in place, the emphasis on employee development, the effectiveness of eHR in affecting business performance, and organization dynamics skills. Thus, the most potent combination of company focuses driving change in HR seems to be a focus on knowledge and competencies combined with a focus on organizational performance.

Second, initiatives are clearly just as important as strategies. Although both strategies and initiatives relate to having a stronger talent strategy, only knowledge and competency initiatives and organizational performance initiatives relate to having a process for high-potential employees. Similarly, an increased emphasis by HR on organizational design and development relates strongly to organizational performance improvement and knowledge initiatives but not to having a knowledge strategy. This emphasis on performance and on knowledge initiatives drives a connection between the talent acquisition and development support from HR and the operational business issues. In short, initiatives are often the vehicle by which companies develop new capabilities, competencies, and ways of functioning. Through these initiatives, HR develops its own expertise and competencies and also is a business partner in helping the organization perform.

Overall, our results clearly show that strategy and change initiatives do make a difference in the way the HR function operates and in its ability to be a successful business partner. When a company explicitly focuses on knowledge and competency and organizational performance capabilities, HR's activities add even greater value and the HR function is more positively regarded. Organizational strategies and initiatives that entail growth and restructuring of the organization and its portfolio of businesses do not relate to these business and strategic support activities.

HR Effectiveness

The next logical question is: What is related to the HR organization's effectiveness? The strongest relationships with effectiveness concern the use of corporate centers of excellence, the rotation of people within HR, centralized processing, and self-service. Also significantly associated are outsourcing transactional work, developing HR systems through joint line-HR task forces, and being a business partner. The factors leading to effectiveness are a combination of approaches that promote efficiency in routine transactional processing and allow HR professionals to focus on expanding their knowledge base, providing expertise, and partnering with others in the businesses. This is a long list of practices but one that provides an actionable agenda for most HR functions. It is also marked by another characteristic: most are practices that are not widely used and that show little increase in use between our 1995 and 2001 surveys. This strongly suggests that one of the reasons that HR is not rated as increasing in effectiveness during this period is that it has not done what it needs to do in order to be perceived as more effective.

The data concerning what determines the effectiveness of the HR organization are clearly consistent with the argument that HR can and should be more of a strategic business partner. The data suggest a number of things that HR can do to become more of a strategic partner. One of them is *not* replacing the head of the HR function with a line manager who has no HR background. HR functions with such leadership are rated as no more effective overall, and they are no more likely to be a strategic partner than HR functions that have leaders with HR backgrounds. One can argue that companies that replace their HR heads with line managers are bringing new perspectives and knowledge to the function, but these companies are also reducing the deep knowledge about HR issues that is potentially the unique contribution of HR to the business table.

Factors that relate to being a strategic partner include the use of service teams, rotation of people in and out of HR, using IT, and placing more emphasis on organizational design and development as well as employee development. Higher levels of organizational dynamics and business skills also are associated with HR being more of a strategic partner. Overall, being a business partner demands high levels of knowledge and skill in HR, as well as organizational designs and practices that link HR managers to business units.

Obstacles to Change

Why hasn't HR changed? There are a number of plausible explanations. One is that there may not have been enough pressure to change. The existing role and activities of HR may be well institutionalized in a kind of codependency relationship. The individuals in the HR function are satisfied with their current role and comfortable delivering services in a traditional mode; recipients of the services are also satisfied with an administrative function that removes what they perceive as onerous HR responsibilities from them, and they are not asking for change. This leads to an institutionalized devaluation of the HR function by the rest of the organization because of HR's low level of contribution to the business. It also makes change difficult because many employees are unwilling to let it change because it serves them.

Ironically, the competition for talent during the last decade of the 1990s may have worked against the upgrading of the HR function. It focused a disproportionate amount of professional HR time on delivering services related to recruiting, orienting, developing, and retaining employees, leaving little time and few resources to spend on activities such as upgrading HR competencies and systems and being a strategic partner. A great deal of HR professionals' time and attention may have been sidetracked by bidding wars for talented employees and by the need to generate and administer reward systems that matched the job market.

A certain service imperative associated with recruiting, developing, motivating, and retaining employees locks the time of most HR professionals into patterns of activity that are difficult to change. Our finding that the amount of attention being paid to almost all HR activities has increased would seem to support the view that even though a consensus is emerging about what constitutes high value-added HR activities, HR professionals find themselves having to spend more time on activities that they know to be low in business value.

Low skill levels in the HR function are an additional compelling explanation for the limited change in the HR function. Just how difficult changing the HR function is becomes apparent when we look at the kinds of skills that members of the HR function must have in order to be rated highly and to play the strategic and business partner roles. HR effectiveness requires a broad range of skills, ranging from relatively routine administrative processing to organizational dynamics and business partner skills. Although business partner and organizational dynamics skills are most highly related to effectiveness, the HR function cannot afford to carry out the core administrative functions ineffectively. Interestingly, HR does not score very highly in administrative skills, especially with respect to managing contractors and IT. These are relatively new competencies that have become important with the transition to eHR.

The more skilled employees in the HR function are in working with others, being team members, coaching, consulting, and leading, the more effective the HR function is. HR effectiveness is clearly related to HR professionals' ability to skillfully influence the performance effectiveness of individuals throughout the organization. For the most part, these are areas in which HR skills are rated the highest.

Business-partnering effectiveness requires knowledge and skills in such areas as change management, strategic planning, and organizational design. These are complex judgmental areas where HR professionals have traditionally had little experience. This expertise is both hard to acquire and in short supply. Becoming expert in business partnering demands the acquisition not only of explicit knowledge but also of tacit knowledge that comes from experience. Applying this expertise demands influencing line management and being part of effective team relationships with others who carry deep knowledge about the business and the market (Mohrman, Finegold, and Klein, forthcoming).

Our data show that although survey respondents see HR professionals as having increased their knowledge of the business since 1995, they are still falling far short in the planning and problem-solving skills required for HR to play a partner role. Understanding the business just gets HR to the table. Expertise in the other areas is required to add value once at the table. Thus, HR is in a bit of a catch-22. HR professionals must get to the table and gain experience in order to gain the knowledge and skills they will need at the table.

Our 2001 survey looked at the application of various approaches to talent management. Particularly prevalent practices are tuition reimbursement programs, involvement of senior management in managing talent, and regular talent reviews. Surprisingly, we found relatively low use of competency systems that are linked to HR practices. We found that although many firms are using e-learning, it is not yet a major vehicle for talent development. Although using IT-based approaches to development relates to being a business partner, this approach appears to be greatly underdeveloped.

Fifty-seven percent of the companies report that they have a special program for high-potential employees. These programs make great use of special development and assessment activities, with less emphasis on employee rotation, mentoring, and coaching. They also make little use of special compensation programs.

Companies appear to be applying a very limited range of approaches to talent development; they seem to be shying away from job rotations and the linking of HR practices to competency systems in order to motivate and provide direction to development experiences. This pattern leads us to believe that HR's difficulty in developing its own competencies may be a microcosm of the larger organization.

Enabling Change

In part, the failure of HR to become a strategic partner may be because it has not yet found a way to deliver high-quality administrative services without devoting a large amount of resources to them. Our data show that eHR offers considerable untapped potential. We found, for example, that the effectiveness of eHR systems in performing HR processes and enabling employee self-service is positively related to how skilled HR is seen to be in providing administrative support. We also found that the most positive outcomes of eHR to date are the efficiency benefits of these systems and that the extent of completeness and integration of these systems relate to overall HR effectiveness. Finally, offering information through an employee portal constitutes a new valued service and relates to HR effectiveness.

Overall, our results suggest that an investment in a high-quality eHR system should increase the HR function's credibility and the perception of the value it adds, while decreasing the time the function spends on administrative tasks. We found some evidence of a substitution effect: providing high-quality systems for administrative processing relates not only to perceived administrative effectiveness but also to perceived effectiveness in all areas. This may be because a high-quality eHR system allows HR staff to spend more time on developing these skills. Furthermore, by offering knowledge and tools to managers and employees through a portal, a high-quality eHR system can provide valuable new services.

eHR has the potential to break the logjam that prevents HR from increasing its competency and changing its business model. In 2001, 83 percent of companies said that they had some form of an eHR system. They most frequently got their eHR systems from an ERP vendor. The data also show that employees frequently have access through employee portals to the Internet and to various kinds of business information.

At this point, the HR function does not perceive eHR systems to be particularly effective. They receive relatively high marks on improving HR services and speeding up HR processes but low marks in areas concerned with HR affecting the business, such as making strategic information available and producing a balanced scorecard of HR's effectiveness. Many companies appear to be investigating and making investments in eHR systems, but in most cases these have not yet proven to be highly effective, nor have they transformed the HR function. Nevertheless, the potential remains for them to be a key delivery vehicle and to make the HR organization much more effective and much more of a business partner.

To summarize, the HR function is changing and is changing in the right direction, but change is slow and not taking place in many of the areas where it is needed. Currently, the HR function is a long way from being a high value-added strategic and business partner that delivers high-quality transactional services in a cost-effective manner. For the function to achieve its potential as a value-adding business and strategic partner, it will have to develop new skills and tools. Additionally, it will have to better deploy its resources to support a redefined role by greatly increasing the exposure of HR professionals to business issues and by employing work structures that bring the HR function together in partnership with the line and other functions. In short, as we will discuss next, it will have to move out of its comfort zone and adopt the processes for the development and motivation of human capital that must characterize knowledge firms.

What does the future hold for the HR function? Three years ago, when we reported on the 1998 data (Lawler and Mohrman, 2000, p. 71), we wrote, "Change has just begun. The next decade will probably see dramatic change in the human resource function in most companies. The opportunity exists for human resource management to become a true strategic partner and to help decide how organizations will be managed, what human resource systems will look like, and how human resource services will be created and delivered."

Our 2001 data suggest that the changes we predicted in our report have not taken place. Yes, change has occurred but not the kind of substantial change that we thought might happen. Fortunately for our credibility as prognosticators, we are still very early in the new decade and the new millennium. HR still has quite a bit of time to change dramatically in many important ways.

If anything, we feel more strongly today about the importance of change in the HR organization. The United States and the developed world are increasingly populated by companies with a higher and higher percentage of employees doing knowledge work. Human capital is becoming increasingly important as a source of competitive advantage, as is intellectual capital. Our research clearly shows that when organizations focus on developing their competencies, capabilities, and knowledge assets, especially when they combine these with a strong focus on their performance capabilities, they make HR much more of a strategic and business partner, and they do make changes in the HR function. Thus, we have good reasons to believe that HR will change.

How will HR be managed and structured in large corporations? Will it still be a large function, employing approximately one out of every hundred employees and organized around its major activities, such as compensation, training, and staffing? We have good reason to believe that it will not. HR needs to look at itself much more as a business, because that is how others in organizations are beginning to look at it. It will be assessed and should assess itself according to whether it adds enough value to justify its costs.

HR as a Business Partner

As a business, HR can have three product lines. The first is the basic HR administrative services and tasks that are involved in compensating individuals, hiring them, training them, and staffing positions in the organization. The second is that of a business partner that helps business units and general managers realize their business plans. In this role, HR needs to provide advice and services concerning organizational development, change management, and the articulation between HR management systems and business operations. It entails leading the development of the human capital and installing HR management practices that position the organization to execute its business plans. The third involves contributing to the organization's strategic direction. It also involves leading the development and assessment of the human capital and the organizational capabilities required to support the organization's long-term success. This business requires individuals in HR who understand business strategy and its relationship to organizational capabilities and core competencies. Let's look separately at how each of the three businesses within HR might develop in the future.

Administrative Services The administrative and functional HR management services of an organization are clearly moving toward being more and more of a commodity that can be delivered in a number of different ways. Historically, these services have been delivered by an in-house HR function in a labor-intensive, poorly integrated, and costly manner. We have little doubt that this labor-intensive approach is obsolete and needs to be replaced by a new model. The obvious replacement technology is a Web-based eHR system. What is unclear at this point is whether the IT self-service systems that companies will use are going to be designed, developed, and delivered by outsourcing vendors or by groups within organizations. Today, at least three models are emerging as ways to use IT to deliver HR services.

The first is the type of custom system that a firm designs for its own use. IT companies including Dell, Cisco, Hewlett-Packard, Microsoft, and Sun Microsystems are currently using these. Some of these systems are very impressive and allow individuals to perform a number of important HR tasks and access a great deal of information on a self-service basis. However, most companies are highly unlikely ever to develop the kind of custom systems that technology companies have developed; the process is simply too expensive and time consuming.

What companies can do, however, is adopt either of two other alternatives: buy an integrated Web-based system sold from a major ERP vendor (for example, PeopleSoft or SAP) or buy individual eHR software applications having to do with compensation administration, staffing, training, and so on from the vendors who are currently selling these. Some good software programs exist that when combined can produce an effective eHR system for companies.

What is still unclear is whether eHR systems will in fact result in a significant increase in the perceived quality of customer service. Will employees feel that the self-service that they get with eHR systems equals or exceeds the quality of service that they get from their current HR representatives? It is also unclear what kind of cost savings eHR systems will generate. Great savings are possible, given the large number of individuals who are currently in HR and the relatively low value added that is contributed by some HR activities such as signing up individuals for insurance coverage, providing information on job openings, and so on.

One final option available to companies is complete business process outsourcing. Exult Inc. is currently the most visible firm providing this outsourcing service. It has signed contracts with a number of major corporations to outsource all of the administrative aspects of their HR management. Promising companies both savings and improved service, it transfers some of the client organizations' HR employees to its payroll and eliminates others. The eliminated employees are replaced by Exult's eHR system. This model is relatively new, so we cannot evaluate its effectiveness, but it is clearly a very different way to deliver HR services and one that has a considerable amount of momentum behind it.

None of the three alternatives for doing HR administration and management will likely be dominant by the end of the decade. But the majority of large firms will very likely use one of these three approaches, because they create the opportunity to build an HR function that is simultaneously more cost-effective and delivers a superior product. In short, they can represent a better business model than the traditional HR model when it comes to delivering routine HR management services and administration.

Business Partner. But what about the business partner activities of HR? Can they be outsourced? Should they be outsourced? Can they be put on the Web? Should they be? Some business partner activities can be greatly enabled by the use of vendors and by the use of the Web. Effective eHR systems can collect, analyze, and report on data about the condition of an organization's human capital in ways that were previously not possible because of the extreme amount of time required to perform these tasks. eHR systems can aid in change management, business plan implementation, and the operations of the business because they can make information readily available to employees and can easily solicit employee feedback and suggestions. But we should point out that computer systems are merely enablers in all these areas—they cannot take the place of human judgment and values in problem solving and decision making.

Many consultants can provide good insights into the implementation of business plans and change management. But our view is that organizations will always need and have skilled generalists to provide many of the services, information, and knowledge that are necessary in order for

HR to be an effective business partner. Playing the partner role entails solving problems and making decisions that involve important values, are highly uncertain, and are context-specific. As a result, they require understanding the business, its strategy, the nature of the workforce, and the required competencies. Taking the partner role entails the application of tacit experience-based knowledge and explicit discipline knowledge, as well as the ability to combine HR knowledge with the perspectives of other disciplines such as business management, marketing, IT, and technology.

The key question here is not whether professional HR executives will need to play the role of business partner, but whether the individuals who are currently HR executives can in fact be effective business partners. The evidence in this study suggests that HR professionals' comfort level is highest with traditional activities and modes of delivery because this is where their effectiveness and skills are the highest. If they want to be effective business partners, they need to change their skill set and become comfortable with a variety of different activities. They need to understand and be able to formulate a business model for the HR function and to contribute to the firm's business model. They need to understand business operations better and be able to craft HR management approaches that fit its requirements. They need to understand organization design, work design, and change management principles and approaches and be able to play a leadership role when the firm considers these issues. Finally, they need to understand different models of staffing, compensation, and other HR practices so that they can effectively implement HR systems that support the organization's business plans.

Strategic Partner. Finally, we look at the strategic partner activities of HR. The rapid rate of change, the need to develop new strategies and to quickly translate them into HR strategies, and the likelihood that the availability of talent will be a key strategic differentiator have greatly increased the importance of HR being a strategic partner. Our view is that this role can only be performed by individuals who have a good understanding of business strategy as well as of HR strategy. Some of the work that is involved in being a strategic partner can be outsourced to HR strategy vendors. But we believe that companies need a strong internal presence of individuals who have good HR knowledge and who can manage the vendors and be truly present at the table when senior executives discuss strategy formulation and implementation.

HR's strategic partner seat at the table needs to be filled by someone who is a senior executive in the corporation, not by a consultant. The importance of this role, and the need to fill it with somebody who understands business, may be one of the reasons why almost 30 percent of HR executives come from the business rather than from the HR function. In essence, some companies may have decided that the HR strategic partner role is too important to leave to someone with an HR background. Our study shows that this is no substitute for developing HR executives who are experts in HR issues and how they affect the business and enable its strategy. Nevertheless, it may be an approach that organizations use more frequently as they try to develop HR as a strategic partner.

The future is likely to provide great opportunities for senior HR managers to be strategic partners. The kind of data that is likely to be available from eHR systems is one of several enablers that can strengthen their position as strategic partners. For example, such a system can help them make significant contributions to strategy formulation because it can provide both cost- and organizational-effectiveness data with respect to HR practices. IT can provide information about what it will take to develop certain key competencies in the workforce and provide data on the existing levels of organizational effectiveness and organizational capabilities. These are all critical to the strategy-planning process. With an eHR system, HR executives will have the opportunity to translate what is known about the existing organization and its capabilities into change programs that will allow the organization to develop the necessary capabilities to implement new strategic plans and new directions.

Thus, the key question with respect to the strategic partner role now is not so much whether it is an important role but how HR can fill that role. As with the business partner role, the question remains whether many of the current individuals in the HR function are capable of filling it. It is not clear whether they understand the business well enough to be a strategic partner. Many of them have never worked outside of HR and as a result have a limited understanding of what the business is about and what the business strategy and HR strategy options are.

HR Organizational Design

A clear organizational model seems to be emerging for companies with multiple business units. It involves creating HR generalists who become the business partner for the line management in business units. This role involves contributing to business unit plans and helping to develop organizational capabilities and implement the HR practices and people development approaches that are needed to create a competent workforce. Business partner generalists are also expected to represent the central HR organization in its dealings with the business unit. Instead of locating many of the HR services in the business unit, multibusiness corporations are creating shared services units and corporate centers of excellence for the business units to draw on. Alternatively, they are outsourcing HR transactional services and telling the business units to use them. The role of the generalist is thus to be both a business partner and a coordinator of HR services to the business unit in which he or she works.

In essence, the HR organization appears to be becoming a type of front-back organization, where the generalist is the front or customer-focused part. The generalist represents the HR organization in the business unit and is responsible for coordinating and delivering services from the back of the organization. The back in this case consists of the shared services units and centers of excellence that are available to the business units and also the services that are outsourced or delivered by HRIS.

Looking Ahead

The opportunity for the HR function to add value at the strategic level is very great, but this is currently more promise than reality. In order for it become reality, two things must happen: (1) HR executives need to develop new skills and knowledge, and (2) HR needs to be able to execute the HR management and administration activities effectively. Doing the basics well is the platform upon which the HR organization needs to build its role as a strategic partner. It is critical because it demonstrates the capacity of the HR function to operate effectively as a business, and it can provide the data and information that enable HR to be an effective strategic partner.

We have articulated the need for a new business model for HR and identified its major feature, but the HR function still appears to be at the very beginning of the changes that are needed in order for that new model to become a reality. Our study has demonstrated that the change process is slower than anticipated, but it has identified a very clear action agenda that can yield an HR function capable of adding more value to the business. We still believe there will be enormous change in the design and operation of HR functions this decade. We have said it before, and we are going to say it again: the HR function needs to look seriously at how it can reinvent itself. The old approaches and models simply are not good enough.

REFERENCES

Arthur Andersen and the Economist Intelligence Unit Executive Briefing. "New Directions in Finance Strategic Outsourcing." 1995.

Becker, B. E., and Huselid, M. A. "High Performance Work Systems and Firm Performance: A Synthesis of Research and Managerial Implications." *Research in Personnel and Human Resources Management,* 1998, *16,* 53–101.

Becker, B. E., and Huselid, M. A. "Overview: Strategic Human Resource Management in Five Leading Firms." *Human Resource Management,* 1999, *38,* 287–302.

Becker, B. E., Huselid, M. A., and Ulrich, D. *The HR Scorecard: Linking People, Strategy, and Performance.* Boston: Harvard Business School, 2001.

BNA. *Human Resource Activities, Budgets, and Staffs.* Washington, D.C.: BNA, 1994.

BNA. *Human Resource Activities, Budgets, and Staffs.* Washington, D.C.: BNA, 2001.

Brockbank, W. "If HR Were Really Strategically Proactive: Present and Future Directions in HR's Contribution to Competitive Advantage." *Human Resource Management,* 1999, *38,* 337–52.

Corporate Leadership Council. *Vision of the Future: Role of Human Resources in the New Corporate Headquarters.* Washington, D.C.: Advisory Board Company, 1995.

Csoka, L. S. *Rethinking Human Resources.* Report Number 1124–95. New York: Conference Board, 1995.

Csoka, L. S., and Hackett, B. *Transforming the HR Function for Global Business Success.* New York: Conference Board, 1998.

Davenport, T. H., and Prusak, L. *Working Knowledge: How Organizations Manage What They Know.* Boston: Harvard Business School, 1998.

Eichinger, B., and Ulrich, D. *Human Resources Challenges: Today and Tomorrow. The First Annual State-of-the-Art Council Report from the Human Resource Planning Society.* New York: Human Resource Planning Society, 1995.

Evans, P. "Business Strategy and Human Resource Management: A Four State Framework." Working paper, INSEAD, Fontainebleau, France, 1994.

Galbraith, J. R. *Designing Organizations.* (2nd ed.) San Francisco: Jossey-Bass, 2002.

Hammer, M., and Champy, J. *Reengineering the Corporation.* New York: Harper Business Press, 1993.

Hitt, M. A., Bierman, L., Shimizu, K., and Kochhar, R. "Direct and Moderating Effects of Human Capital on Strategy and Performance in Professional Service Firms: A Resource-Based Perspective." *Academy of Management Journal,* 2001, *44*(1), 13–28.

Jackson, S., Hitt, M., and DeNisi, A. (eds.). *Managing Knowledge for Sustained Competitive Advantage: Designing Strategies for Effective Human Resource Management.* San Francisco: Jossey-Bass, 2003.

Lawler, E. E. "Strategic Human Resources Management: An Idea Whose Time Has Come." In B. Downie and M. L. Coates (eds.), *Managing Human Resources in the 1990s and Beyond: Is the Workplace Being Transformed?* Kingston, Canada: IRC Press, 1995.

Lawler, E. E. *From the Ground Up.* San Francisco: Jossey-Bass, 1996.

Lawler, E. E., Cohen, S. G., and Chang, L. "Strategic Human Resources Management." In P. Mirvis (ed.), *Building the Competitive Workforce.* New York: Wiley, 1993.

Lawler, E. E., and Galbraith, J. R. "New Roles for the Staff Function: Strategic Support and Services." In J. R. Galbraith and E. E. Lawler (eds.), *Organizing for the Future: The New Logic for Managing Complex Organizations.* San Francisco: Jossey-Bass, 1993.

Lawler, E. E., and Mohrman, S. A. *Creating a Strategic Human Resources Organization.* Los Angeles: Center for Effective Organizations, 2000.

Lawler, E. E., Mohrman, S. A., and Benson, G. S. *Organizing for High Performance: The CEO Report on Employee Involvement, TQM, Reengineering, and Knowledge Management in Fortune 1000 Companies.* San Francisco: Jossey-Bass, 2001.

Lawler, E. E., with Mohrman, S. A., and Ledford, G. E., Jr. *Strategies for High Performance Organizations: The CEO Report.* San Francisco: Jossey-Bass, 1998.

Leonard-Barton, D. *Wellsprings of Knowledge: Building and Sustaining the Sources of Innovation.* Boston: Harvard Business School Press, 1995.

Lepak, D. P., and Snell, S. A. "Managing the Human Resource Architecture for Knowledge-Based Companies." In S. Jackson, M. Hitt, and A. DeNisi (eds.), *Managing Knowledge for Sustained Competitive Advantage: Designing Strategies for Effective Human Resource Management*. San Francisco: Jossey-Bass, 2003.

Lev, B. *Intangibles: Management, Measurement, and Reporting*. Washington, D.C.: Brookings, 2001.

Michaels, E., Handfield-Jones, H., and Axelrod, B. *The War for Talent*. Boston: Harvard Business School Press, 2001.

Mohrman, A. M., and Lawler, E. E. "Human Resource Management: Building a Strategic Partnership." In J. R. Galbraith and E. E. Lawler (eds.), *Organizing for the Future: The New Logic for Managing Complex Organizations*. San Francisco: Jossey-Bass, 1993.

Mohrman, S. A., Cohen, S. G., and Mohrman, A. M., Jr. *Designing Team-Based Organizations*. San Francisco: Jossey-Bass, 1995.

Mohrman, S. A., Finegold, D., and Klein, J. "Designing the Knowledge Enterprise: Beyond Programs and Tools." *Organization Dynamics*, forthcoming.

Mohrman, S. A., Galbraith, J. R., and Lawler, E. E. *Tomorrow's Organization: Crafting Winning Capabilities in a Dynamic World*. San Francisco: Jossey-Bass, 1998.

Mohrman, S. A., Lawler, E. E., and McMahan, G. C. *New Directions for the Human Resources Organization*. Los Angeles: Center for Effective Organizations, 1996.

Mohrman, S. A., Tenkasi, R. V., and Mohrman, A. M., Jr. "Learning and Knowledge Management in Team-Based New Product Development Organizations." In M. M. Beyerlein, D. A. Johnson, and S. T. Beyerlein (eds.), *Advances in Interdisciplinary Studies of Work Teams*. Vol. 5. Greenwich, Conn.: JAI Press, 2000.

Nadler, D. A., Gerstein, M. S., and Shaw, R. B. *Organizational Architecture: Designs for Changing Organizations*. San Francisco: Jossey-Bass, 1992.

Russell, C. *The Master Trend: How the Baby Boom Generation Is Remaking America*. New York: Plenum Press, 1993.

SHRM. *Human Resources Management*. 1998 SHRM/CCH Study. Chicago: CCH, 1998.

Smith, L. H., and Riley, C. F. *Human Resources Alignment Study, Best Prac-*

tices Report: Achieving Success Through People. Houston: American Productivity and Quality Center, 1994.

Ulrich, D. *Human Resources Champions.* Boston: Harvard Business School Press, 1997.

Ulrich, D., Brockbank, W., Yeung, A., and Lake, D. "Human Resource Competencies: An Empirical Assessment." *Human Resource Management,* 1995, *34,* 473–95.

Ulrich, D., Losey, M. R., and Lake, G. (eds.). *Tomorrow's HR Management.* New York: Wiley, 1997.

Waterman, R. "The Seven Elements of Strategic Fit." *Journal of Business Strategy,* 1982, 2(3), pp. 69–73.

Wright, P., and Dyer, L. *State-of-the-Art and Practice Council Report.* New York: Human Resource Planning Society, 2000.

Wright, P., Dyer, L., and Takla, M. *State-of-the-Art and Practice Council Report.* New York: Human Resource Planning Society, 1999.

APPENDIX   *A Survey of the Changing Human Resource Function*

THIS SECTION ASKS DEMOGRAPHIC QUESTIONS ABOUT YOUR COMPANY AND THE HR ORGANIZATION.

---

1. **How many full-time equivalent employees (FTEs, exempt and nonexempt) are part of the HR function? (This number should include both centralized and decentralized staff.)** **234.08**

2. **Of the professional/managerial employees in HR, approximately what percentage are in generalists' roles?** **42.87%**

3. **Of your professional/managerial HR employees, approximately what percent are centralized (for example, corporate staff)?** **46.10%**

4. **What is the background of the current head of HR? (Please check one response.)**

   a. HR management **75.3%**

   b. Other function(s). (Which one[s]?) **24.7%**

5. **How many employees are in your company?** .... (avg.). **21,023**

6. **Is there a union presence in your company?**   a. Yes **(61.1%)**   b. No **(38.9%)**

   If yes, what percentage of your work force is union-represented? **28.03%**

7. **Which of the following best describes your company? (Please check one response.)**

   a. Single integrated business **25.7%**

   b. Multiple related businesses with corporate functions providing some integrative support **38.5%**

   c. Several sectors or groups of business units with some corporate functions and support **26.4%**

   d. Multiple unrelated businesses managed independently in a "holding company" fashion **5.4%**

   e. Other (please specify) _____ **4.1%**

---

8. What percentage of your company's revenue comes from outside the United States? (If your response is 0%, skip to question 11.).......................................**23.50%**

9. What percentage of your company's HR professional employees are located outside the United States? **17.46%**

10. What percentage of your company's employees are located outside the United States?...**25.67%**

THIS SECTION ASKS QUESTIONS ABOUT STRATEGIC INITIATIVES IN YOUR COMPANY.

---

11. To what extent is each of the following strategic initiatives present in your organization?

		Little or No Extent	Some Extent	Moderate Extent	Great Extent	Very Great Extent	Mean
a.	Building a global presence	22	15	19	27	17	3.01
b.	Partnering/networking with other companies	9	31	22	22	16	3.05
c.	Quality	1	7	22	35	35	3.94
d.	Cycle time reduction	9	13	25	36	17	3.39
e.	Accelerating new product innovation	7	9	24	33	28	3.66
f.	Acquisitions	14	23	22	24	17	3.07
g.	Process automation/IT	1	7	27	41	24	3.80
h.	Customer focus	0	3	5	38	54	4.43
i.	Technology leadership	6	13	25	35	22	3.53
j.	Reducing the number of businesses you are in	53	20	16	3	7	1.91
k.	Entering new businesses	28	23	24	17	9	2.56
l.	Talent—being an employer of choice	2	8	28	37	25	3.75
m.	e-Business	5	23	32	32	9	3.18

12. To what extent has each of the following improvement and change initiatives been present in your organization during the past five to seven years?

		Little or No Extent	Some Extent	Moderate Extent	Great Extent	Very Great Extent	Mean
a.	Restructuring	1	5	26	32	35	3.95
b.	Reengineering	5	26	40	16	14	3.08
c.	Downsizing	18	21	26	18	16	2.93
d.	Reducing layers/flattening	8	27	32	20	12	3.01
e.	Team structures	14	26	30	22	7	2.84
f.	Process management	6	19	36	28	12	3.21
g.	Outsourcing	8	31	37	18	5	2.82
h.	Total Quality Management/Six Sigma	27	29	16	19	8	2.50
i.	Employee involvement	5	18	42	23	12	3.18
j.	Cost containment	1	8	16	43	32	3.99
k.	Knowledge/intellectual capital management	9	29	32	21	9	2.92
l.	Employee competency management	7	28	32	23	9	2.99

13. Which of the following best describes the relationship between the HR function and the business strategy of your corporation? (Please check one response.)

a. HR plays no role in business strategy. 3.4%

b. HR is involved in implementing the business strategy. 11.6%

c. HR provides input to the business strategy and helps implement it once it has been developed. 43.8%

d. HR is a full partner in developing and implementing the business strategy. 41.1%

14. For each of the following HR roles, please estimate the percentage of time your HR function spends performing these roles. Please split 100% among the following categories:

PERCENTAGES SHOULD ADD TO 100% FOR EACH COLUMN:	CURRENTLY	5–7 YEARS AGO
a. Maintaining records... (Collect, track, and maintain data on employees)	14.90%	26.75%
b. Auditing/controlling .... (Ensure compliance with internal operations, regulations, legal, and union requirements)	11.41%	17.13%
c. Providing HR services .... (Assist with implementation and administration of HR practices)	31.27%	33.11%
d. Developing HR systems and practices .... (Develop new HR systems and practices)	19.27%	13.86%
e. Strategic business partnering... (Member of the management team; involved with strategic HR planning, organization design, and strategic change)	23.23%	9.05%
TOTAL.......	100 %	100 %*

15. To what extent does each of the following describe the way your HR function is set up to operate?

	Little or No Extent	Some Extent	Moderate Extent	Great Extent	Very Great Extent	Mean
a. Administrative processing is centralized in shared services units.	9	14	23	34	20	3.42
b. Transactional work is outsourced.	24	34	28	13	1	2.34
c. Corporate centers of excellence provide specialized expertise.	13	19	26	30	12	3.10
d. Decentralized HR generalists support business units.	7	4	12	38	39	3.99
e. HR teams provide service and support the business.	5	16	24	37	18	3.49
f. People rotate within HR.	18	26	26	23	8	2.77
g. People rotate into HR.	46	36	13	4	0	1.75
h. People rotate out of HR to other functions.	38	42	16	3	1	1.88
i. Self-funding requirements exist for HR services.	51	23	14	11	1	1.89

Note: May not add to 100 due to rounding error.

		Little or No Extent	Some Extent	Moderate Extent	Great Extent	Very Great Extent	Mean
j.	HR systems and policies are developed through joint line-HR task teams.	5	19	32	32	11	3.25
k.	HR practices vary across business units.	14	38	33	7	7	2.56
l.	Very small corporate staff—most HR managers and professionals are out in businesses.	16	22	26	19	17	2.99
m.	Some activities that used to be done by HR are now done by line managers.	15	37	28	17	3	2.55
n.	Some transactional activities that used to be done by HR are done by employees on a self-service basis.	18	38	24	15	5	2.50
o.	Areas of HR expertise are outsourced.	34	42	17	7	0	1.97

---

16. A. **How has the amount of focus or attention to the following HR activities changed over the past five to seven years as a proportion of the overall HR activity and emphasis?**
   B. **Have any of these activities been partially or completely outsourced?**

		A. ACTIVITY AND EMPHASIS					B. OUTSOURCING			
		Greatly Decreased		Stayed the Same		Greatly Increased	Mean	Not At All	Partially	Completely	Mean
a.	HR planning	0	2	22	45	31	4.05	96	4	0	1.04
b.	Compensation	1	3	26	44	26	3.93	55	44	1	1.46
c.	Benefits	2	8	33	43	14	3.59	19	72	9	1.89
d.	Organization development	1	7	23	42	28	3.89	77	21	2	1.24
e.	Organization design	1	5	32	45	17	3.71	91	8	1	1.09
f.	Strategic planning	2	6	24	44	24	3.82	93	7	0	1.07
g.	Employee training/education	2	9	30	40	19	3.66	26	73	2	1.76
h.	Management development	1	8	22	44	25	3.85	41	59	1	1.60
i.	Union relations	17	16	49	17	1	2.69	86	14	0	1.14
j.	HRIS	1	5	16	45	32	4.01	54	43	3	1.49
k.	Performance appraisal	1	9	30	38	22	3.70	93	6	1	1.08
l.	Recruitment	0	7	29	40	23	3.80	49	50	2	1.53
m.	Selection	0	3	40	40	17	3.70	83	17	1	1.18
n.	Career planning	2	9	55	25	9	3.31	86	14	1	1.15
o.	Employee record keeping	6	29	52	11	1	2.73	73	26	1	1.28
p.	Legal affairs	1	8	56	26	9	3.34	44	51	5	1.60
q.	Affirmative action	3	16	57	18	6	3.06	68	30	2	1.33
r.	Employee assistance	3	11	57	23	5	3.16	20	26	54	2.35
s.	Competency/talent assessment	3	4	29	48	16	3.71	68	31	1	1.33

17. To what extent have you encountered the following problems in managing HR outsourcing/vendors?

		Little or No Extent	Some Extent	Moderate Extent	Great Extent	Very Great Extent	Mean
a.	Resources required to manage the contract and relationship have been more than anticipated.	19	28	30	21	1	2.57
b.	Services haven't been as good as promised.	9	30	39	20	1	2.73
c.	Contractors don't know enough about the company.	17	30	32	18	3	2.59
d.	Cost has been higher than promised.	14	26	39	18	3	2.71
e.	Lack of skills for managing contractors.	29	31	26	10	4	2.30
f.	Loss of competitive advantage from the way we manage people.	53	24	13	8	2	1.82
g.	Negative reaction from business units served.	38	35	19	7	1	1.98
h.	Negative reaction from company employees.	30	40	20	7	2	2.12
i.	Negative reaction from HR employees.	36	33	20	8	2	2.07
j.	Can't have HR systems we need.	40	29	10	14	7	2.20
k.	Switch to new outsourcers is very difficult.	29	30	24	14	3	2.33

SHARED SERVICES (ANSWER ONLY IF YOUR COMPANY HAS MULTIPLE BUSINESS UNITS)

---

18. A. Which of the following services are carried out, at least in part, by central shared services units within your company? (If no service units exist, go to question 19.)
(1 = Not at all, 2 = some aspects a shared service, 3 = handled entirely through a shared service)

B. How effectively are these services performed by your shared services unit?
(1 = Not effectively, 2 = somewhat effectively, 3 = very effectively, 0 = not applicable)

		A. Shared Services				B. Effectiveness of Shared Service Units				
		Not	Some	All	Mean	Not	Somewhat	Very	N/A	Mean
a.	Employee record keeping	23	45	33	2.10	9	28	63	11	2.53
b.	Recruitment and selection	37	50	13	1.76	8	47	45	17	2.37
c.	Career planning	63	23	14	1.50	19	67	13	27	1.94
d.	Organization development and design	47	33	20	1.73	14	55	31	19	2.17
e.	Legal support	18	35	47	2.30	5	22	73	8	2.67
f.	Affirmative action	28	38	34	2.06	12	29	59	14	2.47
g.	Union relations	52	30	18	1.66	13	20	67	30	2.54
h.	Compensation	17	46	37	2.20	5	29	66	7	2.60

Note: **Percentages and mean for B above are computed with N/A (not applicable) responses missing.**

		A. Shared Services				B. Effectiveness of Shared Services Units				
		Not	Some	All	Mean	Not	Somewhat	Very	N/A	Mean
i.	Benefits	9	35	56	2.47	3	36	61	*3*	2.58
j.	Employee training	21	59	19	1.98	6	56	38	*9*	2.33
k.	Management development	32	45	23	1.91	9	53	38	*16*	2.29
l.	HRIS	17	29	54	2.37	11	50	39	*7*	2.28

Note: Percentages and mean for B above are computed with N/A (not applicable) responses missing.

19. To what extent does your talent strategy include the following?

		Little or No Extent	Some Extent	Moderate Extent	Great Extent	Very Great Extent	Mean
a.	A significant investment in e-learning	27	32	21	15	5	2.38
b.	Involvement by senior management	3	22	32	29	14	3.28
c.	Regular talent reviews	10	19	28	27	16	3.21
d.	Competency systems that are linked to HR practices	18	34	25	16	8	2.62
e.	Tuition reimbursement	3	17	27	33	20	3.50
f.	Outplacement/counseling out of lowest performers	16	28	23	23	10	2.82
g.	A corporate university	59	13	14	5	9	1.93

20. Do you have a program that gives special treatment to high-potential employees?

a. Yes **(56.8%)**   b. No **(43.2%) (GO TO QUESTION 22)**

If yes, to what extent does it include the following:	Little or No Extent	Some Extent	Moderate Extent	Great Extent	Very Great Extent	Mean
a. Job rotation programs	15	20	27	29	8	2.94
b. Special incentive programs	44	14	20	15	6	2.25
c. Special development and assessment activities	1	11	43	30	15	3.48
d. Special career development activities	5	12	37	37	10	3.35
e. Mentoring program	12	20	31	30	7	3.00
f. Individualized employment contracts	73	17	2	6	1	1.45
g. Providing a coach	17	31	32	11	10	2.65

21. What percentage of your employees are considered to be high potential? **8.92%**

Item responses are represented in percentages
Mean = average score of responses

22. **Please check the one statement that best describes the current state of your HR processes.**

    a. Completely integrated HR IT system...**7.6%**

    b. Most processes are IT-based but not fully integrated **35.9%**

    c. Some HR processes are IT-based **48.3%**

    d. Little IT present in the HR function **6.9%**

    e. No IT present (GO TO QUESTION 28)...**1.4%**

---

23. **A.** **Can the following activities be done on your company's computer information system by employees and/or managers?**

    B. **How effectively are these being done on your system?**
(1 = Not effectively, 2 = somewhat effectively, 3 = very effectively, 0 = not applicable)

		A. Computer System?				B. Effectiveness?				
		Not at All	Partially	Completely	Mean	Not	Somewhat	Very	N/A	Mean
a.	Salary planning/administration	26	52	22	1.96	7	49	44	13	2.37
b.	Career development planning	63	29	8	1.46	29	57	13	34	1.84
c.	Change benefit coverage	24	33	43	2.19	7	31	62	13	2.55
d.	Change address and/or other personal information	32	27	41	2.09	8	31	62	18	2.54
e.	Apply for a job (external applicants)	23	34	43	2.21	9	47	44	15	2.35
f.	Apply for a job (internal applicants)	22	33	45	2.23	9	39	51	15	2.42
g.	Obtain advice and information on handling personnel issues	56	39	6	1.50	24	59	17	35	1.93
h.	Performance management	30	53	17	1.88	14	59	26	19	2.12
i.	Post job openings	10	26	64	2.54	7	39	54	6	2.47
j.	New-hire orientation	61	34	6	1.45	25	57	18	36	1.93
k.	Travel and expense reimbursements	25	29	46	2.21	15	36	49	15	2.34
l.	Technical skills training	37	54	9	1.72	12	61	27	21	2.15
m.	Scheduling training and development	27	47	26	1.99	10	51	38	14	2.28
n.	Identifying management development resources	51	37	13	1.62	18	62	20	33	2.02
o.	Management development training	55	41	5	1.50	27	63	10	35	1.83
p.	Search for employees with specified skills/competencies	62	30	8	1.47	43	47	11	37	1.68
q.	Purchase products and services from vendors	52	36	12	1.60	20	53	27	32	2.06
r.	Post personal résumé/bio	62	26	12	1.50	40	43	17	36	1.77

Note: **Percentages and mean for B above are computed with N/A (not applicable) responses missing.**

Item responses are represented in percentages
Mean = average score of responses

24. **Which of the following best describes how you developed your eHR system?**

    a.   No system (IF NO, GO TO QUESTION 28)... **17.0%**

    b.   Developed it ourselves **19.0%**

    c.   Obtained it from our ERP vendor (for example, PeopleSoft) **37.4%**

    d.   Purchased most or all of it from vendors (ASPs) who provide pieces of an HR system......... **15.0%**

    e.   Hired a consulting firm to design it.. **4.1%**

    f.   Outsourced its design and operation to a consulting firm **1.4%**

    g.   Other (please specify): _____ **6.1%**

---

25. **To what extent are the following available to employees through an employee portal:**

	Little or No Extent	Some Extent	Moderate Extent	Great Extent	Very Great Extent	Mean
a. Company strategic and performance information	28	20	21	22	9	2.63
b. Industry and competitor information	40	26	20	14	0	2.07
c. Executive messages to employees	11	12	24	28	25	3.46
d. Access to technical knowledge and resources	19	29	20	21	10	2.74
e. Access to market knowledge	31	30	19	17	2	2.29
f. Access to knowledge experts	39	31	23	4	3	2.02
g. Access to knowledge communities	45	27	16	10	2	1.98
h. Open access to Internet	6	9	12	31	41	3.92
i. A manager's tool kit	27	23	19	21	10	2.65
j. Life event–focused HR processes	32	24	23	12	10	2.45

26. **Have you developed an eHR personal portal for most or all of your employees?**

    a. Yes **(41%)** b. No **(59%)**

27. **To what extent do you consider your eHR system to**

	Little or No Extent	Some Extent	Moderate Extent	Great Extent	Very Great Extent	Mean
a. Be effective	14	26	44	14	2	2.63
b. Satisfy your employees	20	30	37	12	1	2.43
c. Improve HR services	9	22	31	33	5	3.02
d. Build employee loyalty	36	38	20	4	2	1.98
e. Reduce HR transaction costs	13	27	29	21	10	2.88
f. Alienate employees	65	30	4	1	1	1.43
g. Provide new strategic information	31	37	21	11	0	2.11

		Little or No Extent	Some Extent	Moderate Extent	Great Extent	Very Great Extent	Mean
h.	Support strategic change	27	33	23	14	3	2.33
i.	Speed up HR processes	10	23	26	29	12	3.09
j.	Reduce the number of employees in HR	25	31	26	14	4	2.42
k.	Support organizational growth	19	36	28	14	3	2.48
l.	Integrate different HR processes (for example, training, compensation)	29	25	29	13	3	2.37
m.	Enable the analysis of HR's impact on the business	39	29	16	13	3	2.09
n.	Produce a balanced scorecard of HR's effectiveness	47	25	14	13	1	1.95
o.	Enable analysis of workforce characteristics	26	29	21	18	6	2.48
p.	Provide a competitive advantage	31	35	18	14	2	2.20

---

28. How satisfied are you with the skills of your current HR professional/managerial staff?

		Very Dissatisfied	Dissatisfied	Neutral	Satisfied	Very Satisfied	Mean
a.	Team skills	0	9	25	59	7	3.65
b.	Functional HR expertise	0	7	15	53	25	3.96
c.	Business understanding	0	20	35	37	9	3.34
d.	Interpersonal skills	0	4	10	69	17	3.99
e.	Cross-functional experience	1	36	44	16	3	2.84
f.	Consultation skills	2	15	37	39	7	3.35
g.	Record keeping	0	7	29	51	13	3.70
h.	Coaching and facilitation	1	12	33	48	5	3.44
i.	Leadership/management skills	1	14	40	40	5	3.33
j.	Managing contractors/vendors	1	15	43	31	9	3.32
k.	Global understanding	7	36	40	16	2	2.70
l.	Organization design	3	31	45	19	2	2.85
m.	Strategic planning	5	30	41	20	4	2.89
n.	IT	4	19	42	31	4	3.11
o.	Change management	2	23	37	35	3	3.15

29. What percentage of your companywide professional/managerial HR staff possesses the necessary skill set for success in today's business environment? (Circle one.)   Mean: 4.25

0	4.7	18.9	33.1	33.1	10.3	0
None	Almost None	Some	About Half	Most	Almost All	All
0%	1-20%	21-40%	41-60%	61-80%	81-99%	100%

Item responses are represented in percentages
Mean = average score of responses

30. In view of what your company needs, how effective is the HR organization in each of the areas below. Please rate the activities on a scale of 1 to 10 by circling the appropriate number. If NOT APPLICABLE, circle N/A.

		1	2	3	4	5	6	7	8	9	10		Not Applicable	Mean
A.	**Providing HR services**													
	Not meeting needs	0	0	1	2	7	12	27	37	12	2	All needs met	0	7.33
B.	**Providing change consulting services**													
	Not meeting needs	1	4	9	11	18	18	17	15	4	2	All needs met	1	5.74
C.	**Being a business partner**													
	Not meeting needs	0	1	5	13	9	21	24	15	10	3	All needs met	0	6.41
D.	**Developing organization skills and capabilities**													
	Not meeting needs	1	5	5	12	11	23	21	14	7	1	All needs met	0	5.99
E.	**Tailoring HR practices to fit business needs**													
	Not meeting needs	0	3	3	5	10	21	27	18	10	3	All needs met	0	6.67
F.	**Helping shape a viable employment relationship for the future**													
	Not meeting needs	0	2	5	9	11	26	19	17	13	0	All needs met	0	6.40
G.	**Managing outsourcing of transactional services (for example, benefits)**													
	Not meeting needs	0	1	7	12	12	17	17	21	9	4	All needs met	8	6.42
H.	**Managing outsourcing of HR expertise (for example, compensation design)**													
	Not meeting needs	2	4	10	12	13	15	16	18	7	4	All needs met	13	5.98
I.	**Operating centers of excellence**													
	Not meeting needs	2	4	11	12	21	14	14	10	9	2	All needs met	15	5.61
J.	**Operating shared services units**													
	Not meeting needs	3	4	6	12	17	10	20	18	10	1	All needs met	17	6.02
K.	**Helping to develop business strategies**													
	Not meeting needs	1	3	11	11	16	19	19	12	7	1	All needs met	0	5.78
L.	**Being an employee advocate**													
	Not meeting needs	0	1	3	5	8	11	24	27	17	5	All needs met	0	7.20
M.	**Change management**													
	Not meeting needs	2	3	8	13	9	19	18	21	6	2	All needs met	0	6.06